The
On-High
Calling

The On-High Calling

The On-High Calling
All *new* material in this edition
copyrighted by SeedSowers Publishing House
Printed in the United States of America
All rights reserved

Published by The SeedSowers
P.O. Box 3317
Jacksonville, FL 32206
1-800-228-2665

Library of Congress Cataloging - in - Publication Data

Sparks, T. Austin
The On-High Calling / T. Austin-Sparks
ISBN 0-94023284-7
1. Spiritual Life   1. Title

Times New Roman 12pt

The
On-High
Calling

by
T. Austin-Sparks

Preface

T. Austin-Sparks is one of the great figures of the twentieth century who ministered outside of the organized church. For over forty years he held forth at Honor Oak in London, England. The conferences he spoke at, both in Europe and America, have had a profound influence on our time.

Brother Sparks published over one hundred books and pamphlets. The majority of them have ceased to be available to the Christian family. This has been a great loss, as the content of his message has placed him in the category of only a few men of the last one hundred years.

T. Austin-Sparks and Watchman Nee, more than any other men, have influenced the lives of believers who are outside traditional churches. We have felt very strongly that all of brother Sparks' books and pamphlets should be brought back into print if at all possible.

Read T. Austin-Sparks. It is our hope that in republishing his works, his ministry will take wings again, and the influence of his word will spread across the English-speaking world. Hopefully this will give his message a greater influence than ever before.

We send this book forth with a prayer that what he ministered will become realties in the 21st century.

The SeedSowers

CHAPTER ONE

THE PURPOSE OF COMPANIONS

"Wherefore, holy brethren, partakers of a heavenly calling" (Hebrews iii. 1).

"For we are become partakers of Christ, if we hold fast the beginning of our confidence firm unto the end" (Hebrews iii. 14).

OUR FIRST THING to do is to consider briefly the one word which is going to stand over all our meditations. It is the word which occurs in each of the verses above cited: the word 'partakers'. The Greek word so translated occurs some five times in this Letter to the Hebrews: i. 9; iii. 1, 14; vi. 4; xii. 8. In Luke v. 7 it is translated 'partners', and other translations are 'fellows', 'companions'. There are also other variations of the same original word or root.

Having looked carefully into the original meaning I have come to the conclusion that its truest and deepest meaning is 'companions'. Therefore I have taken this to define and govern all that we shall consider in these chapters. 'Companions of Christ': 'Companions of a heavenly calling'.

This idea of 'companions' runs right through the Bible as being the ultimate thought of God concerning man, and man's relationship to Him. Behind everything that is official in relationships to the Lord there is always a personal element. Think of Abraham! Abraham was a great servant of the Lord and he served Him very faithfully. But the deepest thing about Abraham was that he was God's friend. God spoke of him as *"My friend"* (Isaiah xli. 8). That carries with it this idea of a 'companion of God'.

Moses was a great servant of the Lord, and the Lord often spoke of him as 'Moses my servant'. But we know that there was something deeper in it than that—*"The Lord spake unto Moses face to face, as a man speaketh unto his friend"* (Exodus xxxiii. 11). There was a very intimate relationship between God and Moses and Moses and God. In reality Moses was a 'companion of the Lord'.

And what about David? There are many things said about him, but the greatest was that God said he was a man *"after my heart"* (Acts xiii. 22). That is the meaning of a companion of the Lord.

When the Lord Jesus came on to this earth He chose His disciples and apostles on the basis of companionship. Call them 'disciples', if you like—those who had to enter the school of Christ and be taught. Call them 'apostles'—those who were to be sent forth by Him. But the deepest thing in their relationship to Him was that they were His companions. Toward the end of their time He said: *"Ye are they which have continued with me in my temptations"* (Luke xxii. 28). They were His companions in life and His companions in suffering. He said: *"Ye are my friends"* (John xv. 14).

When we come to the Church, it is not some official, ecclesiastical institution. That is very cold, very formal and very distant. But when the Lord speaks about His Church it is always in terms of love: *"The church of God which he purchased with his own blood"* (Acts xx. 28)— *"Christ also loved the church, and gave himself up for it"* (Ephesians v. 25). Perhaps we have to recover this idea about the Church: it is called to be the 'companion of

Christ'. Its deepest relationship with Him is a heart relationship—just to be His companions in life, in work, in suffering and in glory.

Having said a word about the idea of companions, let us go on to think of the *purpose* of companions. The Bible is a book of one purpose, and that one purpose lies behind all its stages and phases. It lies behind creation, behind divine foreknowledge, behind election, behind the persons whom God chose, behind all the movements of God through the Bible, behind all the figures and all the types and behind the three main sections of the Old Testament—the section of priesthood, followed by the section on kingship and then followed by the section of the prophets. Those three sections comprise the Old Testament and this one purpose lies behind everything in the Old Testament. God is revealed in the Bible as a God of purpose, and every movement in His sovereignty is governed by this one purpose.

What is this one purpose in and through all? It is centred in God's Son. In all things God had His Son alone in view. The 'all things' is a very comprehensive term, but all is comprehended in God's Son. As we are going to dwell very much in this Letter to the Hebrews, take note of this very factor at the beginning of it.

The first great statement is concerning all God's past ways and methods. In times past God moved by this means and that means, in this way and that way, but at the end of those times He concentrates all in His Son. He gathers all that up together and focuses it in His Son. The Son of God comprehends the whole of the Old Testament and all God's ways in the Old Testament. To emphasize that, this Letter goes on through the first two chapters to bring the greatness of God's Son into view. You know the wonderful things said about God's Son in the first chapter. Here is the One who is above all others, who comprehends all else in the thought of God.

So God's interest in His Son is brought before us right at the beginning, and the declaration is that God's purposes are all centred in His Son. That Son is now known unto men as Jesus Christ. But the point here is this: Having introduced and presented the Son, and having magnified Him, the Holy Spirit, through the writer, goes on in this way (and there ought to be no break in chapters here) 'Wherefore—for this reason, because of this, because of God's purpose concerning His Son, because of the infinite greatness of the Son, greater than all others and all else—holy brethren, you are called into companionship with God's Son and companionship in the heavenly calling of God's Son.'

We come to our third point in this connection. There are two principles related to divine purpose throughout the Bible. The first is what we have just pointed out: God works ever and always and only in relation to His purpose. The statement of the Apostle Paul about God is: *"(He) worketh all things after the counsel of his will"* (Ephesians i. 11), and that will is centred in His Son. He therefore works ever, always and only in relation to His Son.

The Bible contains almost uncountable things. What a great mass of *things* there are in the Bible! Things which God created and things which God used. And then what a lot of persons there are that God laid His hand upon! A whole multitude of them. And then how many are the different ways that God went to realize His purpose! The ways of God are very many. The means that He employed—the Bible is just full of these things. And then we have God's blessings. God is very often found blessing people and blessing things. On the other hand, there are the judgments of God. He is a God of judgment and the Bible contains many of the judgments. But when we have said all that (and, of course, we could never really comprehend all that—this Book is always far, far too big for us!), not one of these things, persons, means used, blessings or judgments or anything else is a thing in itself. If God is the God of creation, if He chooses men, if He uses things, if He blesses or judges, He always does so with one object in view. He created all things for His Son. That is a definite Bible statement. He took hold of these persons with His Son in view. It was so with Abraham, and through Abraham we come to God's Son, 'after the flesh'.

Well, let us be content with making the statement. If God blessed, it was because that thing stood right in line with His Son's interests. If we want the blessing of the Lord we must get alongside of the Lord Jesus and be wholly committed to Him. The Father never sees us apart from the Lord Jesus, and it is in Him that the blessing of God is to be found. If the Bible has much to say about divine judgments—and how much is said by the prophets about the judgments of God!—it is because things then were contrary to His interests in His Son. God always keeps His eye focused upon His one object and that object is His Son. God wastes nothing. He is not just interested in little things as such. The little things become very big things with God when they are related to His Son. Are you a very little person? Very unimportant? If you are vitally related to His Son God looks upon you as very important. But it is not your importance, nor mine. It is the importance of His Son.

This is true about any faithful school-teacher. I suppose all of us have been to school and have had our school-teachers, and some of us in our school-days did want to stand well with our teachers. We tried to please them because we wanted to be happy with our teachers and we wanted to get all that the teachers could do for us. But my recollection of school-masters is this: They did not have *me* in view. The only thing they had in view where I was concerned was how their object was going to be realized. They had to have good scholars who passed examinations and came out top, and everything that they thought of related to that end. Sometimes they would be very pleasant to me, and then I thought 'What a good boy am I!' Sometimes it was the other way and I knew something about the judgments of school-teachers! Now this was not because they liked me or disliked me. What they really did like was the end when the examinations came, and everything about me was looked at in the light of the one object.

While we do not like to call God a school-master, the principle is the same. He is looking at us in the light of His Son: 'How does that man or that woman answer to My thought about My Son? How much of My Son is there in that man or in that woman?' Later we shall see how God works on that ground; but note: this is a principle in God's purpose. That leads us to the second principle.

While God is a God of purpose, ever moving in relation to that purpose, going on, no matter what happens, with His purpose, working on the ground of His own sovereign lordship, no man being able to prevent Him, He is going to reach His end. That is why He has given us the Book of the Revelation. Before we reach the end He has told us what it is going to be like. His purpose is going to be realized. Nevertheless, He keeps to this other principle—He always retains man in a place of responsibility. He never lets man off from responsibility. Why is that? Because His purpose in His Son is to be realized in man, the great, corporate man in which Christ is to have His fulness. Christ is not going to realize God's purpose alone. He will not be in glory just as one isolated unit. So we come back to our verse: "Holy brethren, *companions* of a heavenly calling . . . we are become *companions* of Christ, if we hold fast. . . ."

Paul says that the Church is "*the fulness of him that filleth all in all*" (Ephesians i. 23). Hence there is a responsibility resting upon man, and no book in the Bible emphasizes that more than the Letter to the Hebrews. In that connection this Letter is one of the most terrible Letters in the Bible. On the one side it is the most glorious thing, and on the other side it is the most terrible thing. We shall be seeing that more fully as we go on.

At this point it is very important for us to recognize another matter, and this is what comes out in this Letter. Indeed, it is going to be the thing which governs all our consideration through these days. If God takes up a vessel in relation to His purpose—it may be individuals, or it may be a company of people, like Israel, or like the men whom God took up in the Bible—and that vessel does not respond to God's will, God will pass by that vessel and find another. He will call in others to take its place.

The greatest instance of this is seen in Israel. God chose Israel to be the vessel through which He would bring in His Son. Israel was called and chosen of God in relation to His Son and His purpose in His Son. And what did Israel do with God's Son? They refused Him, and therefore they refused God's purpose, so God put them aside and passed on. Jesus said: "*The kingdom of God shall be taken away from you, and shall be given to a nation bringing forth the fruits thereof*" (Matthew xxi. 43).

That is the very meaning of the Letter to the Hebrews,

B

as we shall see. No one can say of Israel now: 'They are the companions of Christ.' Israel was once the companion of God, but the companion of God failed God.

What a lot of light this throws upon the fact that the Lord Jesus called Judas amongst the twelve! He was one of the twelve, called to be a companion, and he betrayed his Lord. Israel was called to be the companion of God and Christ, and Israel betrayed the Son of God—a companion set aside, rejected, while God goes on with His purpose and brings in others to take Israel's place.

So this explains the wonderful Letter to the Hebrews. It is the Letter of the place and of the greatness of Jesus Christ. It sets forth the wonder of being called to be a companion of Christ, and then it makes it so clear what a terrible thing it is for those who are called to be companions to fail the Lord. It says: "*How shall we escape, if we neglect so great salvation?*" (Hebrews ii. 3). You can never understand that phrase 'so great salvation' until you understand what it means to be a companion of Christ. Is there anything greater than being a companion of Jesus Christ? When you think of who He is, and of all that God has purposed concerning Him—and then to think that you and I are called to be companions of that Son of God! That is indeed a very great salvation! It is the 'so great salvation'.

We have spent our time just going round this one word 'companion'. The New Testament is built around that one word and around the one idea of companions of Christ. Christ is first seen choosing His companions, and then He is seen teaching them by word and by deed. Then He is seen testing and sifting them. Are they true companions? Or are they only associated with Him for what they are going to get from Him? You can have plenty of companions if you give them everything and if they can get all that they want from you. But what about the day when you can give them nothing but suffering? And persecution, and everything that is against their natural interests? You can only offer them a place in the Father's house! So He sifted them, He tested them, and on more than one occasion it is said " . . . *many of his disciples went back, and walked no more with him*" (John vi. 66). Companionship is something which is tested and sifted through adversity. So if you have an extra lot of testing and of suffering in your relationship with Christ, remember that He is seeking to have us as His closest companions, in fellowship with Himself, not only in His glory, but in His sufferings.

So the relationship with Christ is on the basis of fellowship. Oneness in life, in purpose, in experience, in discipline, in death, burial and resurrection, in anointing and then, at last, oneness with Him in His heavenly glory.

We must realize that Jesus is repeating Himself in a spiritual way in this dispensation. When Luke wrote the Book of the Acts, he commenced with these words: "*All that Jesus began both to do and to teach*" (Acts i. 1). His implication was: 'I am now going to write what He is going on doing and teaching. It is the same Jesus. He is doing the same work and doing the same things, but there is a difference. Before it was by illustration in a temporal way. Now it is the meaning of those things in a spiritual way. The meaning that was in the things then is now in what He is doing with us in a spiritual way. Did He open physically blind eyes? He is now opening spiritually blind eyes, and that is much more important.'

This same Jesus is going on with the same work in meaning now with you and with me. He is repeating His earthly life in a spiritual way. He is more on the line of meaning than of acts now.

Why do we say that? Well, when we were children we used to sing a hymn (and I think when we are grown up we often feel the same!):

"I think when I read that sweet story of old,
    When Jesus was here among men, ¦
How He called little children as lambs to His fold:
    I should like to have been with them then."

Do you feel that you would have liked to have lived with Him then, on the earth? Is that the best thing that you can think about? Let me tell you that you have something far better than that now! That same Jesus is with us, but, oh! on a much more wonderful basis than He was then. And we are called *now* to be companions of Christ and companions of the heavenly calling. His dealings with us, perhaps, are far more real because they are spiritual and eternal, while His dealings when He was on earth were only physical, and for the time being. It is a good thing to look after people's bodies and to help them in this life, but there is something very much more than that. It is that heavenly calling, that which is eternal, that which will not pass as our life work when time is no more—*"Wherefore, holy brethren, companions of a heavenly calling . . . we are become companions of Christ if we hold fast"*.

All that is only by way of laying a foundation. As the Lord helps we shall build on that foundation.

CHAPTER TWO

WHO ARE THE COMPANIONS?

WE COME NOW to a more general look at the Letter in which our particular occupation is found, which particular matter we believe to be *the* concern of the Letter: the Letter to the Hebrews.

In the oldest manuscripts the title is just simply 'To the Hebrews', but we understand that to mean Hebrew Christians, or Christians who naturally were Hebrews.

We must understand the setting of the Letter in New Testament times. We know of the great battle which raged then between Jews and Christians. The Apostle Paul, who was himself a great Hebrew, had a very large heart for his own people. Do you remember what he said? "*I could wish that I myself were anathema from Christ for my brethren's sake, my kinsmen according to the flesh*" (Romans ix. 3). He was prepared to let everything go if only his people would accept the Lord Jesus, so great was his desire and his hope for them. But he fought a losing battle for Israel, and in the last chapter of the Book of the Acts you see Paul's surrender of that hope: "*Be it known therefore unto you, that this salvation of God is sent unto the Gentiles: they will also hear*" (Acts xxviii. 28). In effect he said: 'Seeing that Israel will not hear, we will give them up. I give up my great hope for them and I turn to those who will hear—I turn to the Gentiles.'

Then you come to this Letter to the Hebrews, and at the end of it you have the result of Israel's refusal. The writer makes this appeal to these Hebrew Christians: *"See that ye refuse not him that speaketh. For if they escaped not, when they refused him that warned them on the earth, much more shall not we escape, who turn away from him that warneth from heaven: . . . And this word, Yet once more, signifieth the removing of those things that are shaken, as of things that have been made, that those things which are not shaken may remain. Wherefore, receiving a kingdom that cannot be shaken"* (Hebrews xii. 25, 27, 28).

These words contain the final judgment upon the Hebrews who rejected Christ. That 'shaking' referred, in the first instance, to the destruction which was coming upon Israel in the year A.D. 70, and when that happened Israel was left without a country, without a city, without a temple and without a government. Everything was shaken until it fell completely—the result of refusing to hear *"him that warneth from heaven"*.

It is in that setting that we have this Letter to the Hebrews. On the one side it is a final appeal to the Hebrew Christians not to go back from Jesus Christ. On the other side the Letter is a great warning as to what will happen if they do. So you have to put this Letter right into that setting: it is set in a great crisis of spiritual life, and, of course, it contains an abiding message for all time.

Let us look for a minute at the three features which made up that great conflict and which led to that final division.

The first feature was Christ Himself, as the Messiah, and Jesus as the Christ. Of course, the Jews believed in a Christ, for 'Christ' is only the Greek word for the Hebrew 'Messiah'. But the trouble was that they would not have Jesus as the Messiah, and so, as was prophesied, Jesus became the stone upon which they fell and were broken to pieces. It was a matter of the place they gave to Jesus.

You can see into what a high place this letter puts Jesus, and we are going to see that again presently. Jesus was God's anointed Son, the Christ, the Rock upon which they were broken. That was the first great factor in the conflict and in the ultimate division.

We must always remember that the test of everyone and everything is the place which is given to Jesus Christ. If anyone ever comes to you wanting you to accept some system of teaching, having wonderful arguments and using a lot of the Bible, what are you going to do about it? You may not be able to meet their arguments, and you may not even be able to answer Scripture with Scripture, but there is one thing that will always go to the heart of the matter: 'What place do you give to the Lord Jesus Christ? Do you give Him the place of God's eternal Son?' Everything stands or falls on that. You can try it, and you will find that most of the false teachers will begin to wriggle on that: 'Oh, we believe in Jesus as a great man, as the greatest teacher that ever lived', and so on, 'but if you want us to believe that Jesus is God, well, we just cannot go that far.' It is the place given to the Lord Jesus that is the test of everyone and everything.

That is the first factor in this great conflict in the Letter to the Hebrews, and you will see why the writer uses the whole of the first part to magnify the Lord Jesus.

The second feature is what the writer here speaks of as 'the heavenly calling', and you have to put all the emphasis upon that word 'heavenly'. You see, the Hebrews wanted an earthly calling: and all who are like them, even if they are called Christians, just want an earthly calling; a Christianity that belongs to this earth and to this world. We are going to enlarge upon this later, but there is a tremendous significance in this little phrase 'the heavenly calling'.

Then there was this third feature. These Hebrews were prepared to be Christians, but it must be a Christianity after their own mind. It must be a Christianity that allows the Old Testament system to continue. It must allow Moses to continue. It must allow all the law of Moses to continue. It must allow the temple to continue. It must allow all the Old Testament priests to continue. It must allow all the sacrifices to continue—'We are prepared to be Christians if you will let us bring over our Old Testament into Christianity, but if you say all that is finished and a *heavenly* system has taken its place, then we cannot have that.' They wanted the Jewish system brought into Christianity, that is, a Christianity of ritual and form. Do you see the force of this word 'Companions of a heavenly calling'? 'Companions of Christ'?

These companions of Christ are those who are constituted anew on a heavenly and spiritual basis. They are the ones who are responding to a *heavenly* calling.

Now we have come to the point of the transition from the natural and earthly Israel to the new spiritual and heavenly Israel. This transition ought to have been in a divine sequence, the one quietly giving way to the other. The old ought to have made full place for the new. The old Israel ought to have died, been buried and raised again in Christ and become the heavenly Israel—the companions of Jesus Christ—but they refused to have it like that. And because they refused to have it like that they were set aside. God is just moving on with His purpose concerning His Son, and, although many were called, few were chosen. There were a few of Israel who were chosen as companions, but the many who were called refused, and so they were set aside, and God

 موved in this transition toward His new heavenly Israel.

Note: they *positively* refused to move on to heavenly ground. They refused to move on to the ground of the heavenly Man. Hence, as a result, they went the way of Adam—and here is a very interesting and instructive thing.

Adam was made by God, chosen by God and called by God into relation to His purpose concerning His Son, but when Adam was made he was not perfect. He was innocent, but he was not perfect. You know the difference between being innocent and being perfect! A little baby child is innocent, but will you say that it is perfect? No, it is not perfect. It has to grow up, and it will only grow up and become perfect as it goes through all sorts of difficulties and troubles. We call them 'growing pains', and that is the way of becoming perfect from an innocent child to a full-grown man. Adam was innocent, like a little child. He was very beautiful, with no sin in him, but he was not perfect. He had to come to spiritual perfection. He had still to be made like God's Son. That is what he was created for. God allowed him to be tested, and, oh, what a wonderful thing would have happened if Adam had gone through his testing triumphantly! From the innocence of a little child he would have become a spiritually full-grown man like the Lord Jesus *humanly*, and we, the children of Adam, would have been very different people. But he failed in his test and did not go the way to which God had called him. What did God do? He put Adam aside. He put a curse upon him and said, in effect: 'That kind of being can never satisfy Me. He has refused to go the way of My Son.'

That is exactly what happened to Israel after the flesh. God made Israel, chose Israel and called Israel—all with

His Son in view. And Israel refused to go God's way. Israel was tested as to Jesus Christ—the four Gospels are just full of Israel being tested concerning Jesus Christ, and they all close with Israel saying 'No!' to God's way. So God did with Israel as He did with Adam—He put them aside. He put a curse upon them and for these many centuries that curse has rested upon Israel.

In this Letter, you see, you have that possibility presented. God is saying to the Hebrew Christians 'Do not refuse Him that speaketh from heaven.' But here is the other side of the story. Israel positively refused God's heavenly calling . . . and just at that point God's *eternal* plan is revealed, that is, a heavenly people with a spiritual nature occupying a place in God's creation. That is what God eternally intended. He intended that before He called Israel, and He called Israel to be a people like that—a heavenly people with a spiritual nature.

The point is that just here, when Israel refuses, God presents His *eternal* plan, which is a heavenly people of a spiritual nature.

The whole of the New Testament is the body of truth which relates to this *eternal* will of God. Let us just look at that very hurriedly. We will take the four Gospels. (No! We are not going to study the four Gospels! We are just going to look at them.)

If you take up Matthew, Mark, Luke and John and get some idea of what they contain, and then stand back from them, you are able to see two lines of movement right through them. These two movements run along-side of each other.

On the one side there is the Jewish idea of the Messiah and the Jewish idea of the kingdom of God. The whole Jewish system is there.

Alongside of that, and over against it, there is something that is different. There is God's idea, and heaven's idea, of the Messiah. That is very different from the Jewish idea, and it is always in conflict with the Jewish idea. Then there is God's idea, and heaven's idea, of the kingdom of God, and it is very different from the Jewish idea.

There is the Jewish idea of the king running along one side through the four Gospels—what kind of a king they want and are determined to have. Alongside of it, and over against it, is God's idea, and heaven's idea, of a king: *"Behold, thy king cometh unto thee . . . lowly, and riding upon an ass"* (Zechariah ix. 9). That is not the Jewish idea of a king! 'How can a meek man riding on an ass overthrow the mighty Roman Empire? That is not our idea of a king . . . *"We will not that this man reign over us"* (Luke xix. 14)'.

So, you see, the two lines run through the four Gospels: the Hebrew idea and the heavenly idea. That is the very meaning of the four Gospels. When you get to the end of them you have the Jewish idea rejected fully and finally by God, and, on the other side, God's idea introduced and established for ever.

Two thousand years have proved that. The one side of an earthly system has gone and there has been nothing of it for two thousand years. On the other side there is God's idea of His kingdom. That was introduced when Israel was rejected, and God has been going on with that for two thousand years. We have God's King; we are in God's Kingdom; we are under God's government.

That is what the four Gospels say to us. Of course, that is not all, but that is the general conclusion of the four Gospels. Later on we are going to see the details in the Gospels, or, at least, in one of them, which will show how true that was. These four Gospels show the rejection by

God of those who rejected His Son, and on the other side they show God bringing in that which was according to His Son and establishing it for ever so that the very gates of hell have not been able to prevail against it.

You move from the Gospels to the Book of the Acts, and here you have two features. First of all, you have the feature of transition from the old to the new. With God the transition is complete, but with His people it is made slowly because they are not ready to accept it. It was slower than it ought to have been because James, the head of the church in Jerusalem, still wanted to have something of old Israel, and even Peter was very reluctant to abandon Israel and go right out to the Gentiles. And dear Barnabas was caught in that snare. Paul says, with grief in his heart, "*even Barnabas*" (Galatians ii. 13). These who were of the old tradition were very slow to give up their tradition, but you see that God is going on—'James, Peter, or whoever it may be, if you are not coming on I am going on, and if you are not going on I shall leave you behind and find others.' And while they were so slow He brought in Paul—and Paul got things going. The transition was complete with Paul, and he was God's instrument for completing the transition. The Letter to the Galatians is the instrument by which that transition was completed. Judaism in the Christian church received a fatal blow with that Letter.

You pass from the Book of the Acts to the Letters—what are called the 'Epistles'—and what have you here? Just the full body of teaching concerning the heavenly and spiritual nature of the people of God. It is applied to a whole variety of connections. There is one state of things in Corinth and another state of things in Galatia, and yet another in Ephesus, and so on. But applied to all these different conditions is this one thing: it is God's intention to have a heavenly and spiritual people. All the Letters were applied to different situations with that one object in view. Every Letter in the New Testament has something to say about this heavenly nature of the people of God.

We arrive at the Letter to the Hebrews, and this Letter takes a very, very important place in this whole question, as it is a summary of the whole New Testament. In it is gathered up the whole meaning of the New Testament, and into it there flow tributaries, making it the meeting place of all the revelation of God concerning His Son, Jesus Christ.

What is God's purpose concerning His Son? "Wherefore, holy brethren, *companions* of a heavenly calling . . . we are become *companions* of Christ." Who are the companions of Christ? Those who have fully left the whole earthly realm of things and are joined to the heavenly Lord: those who have become God's spiritual Israel: those who have answered to the heavenly calling. Paul cried, when he was on trial: "*Wherefore, O king Agrippa, I was not disobedient unto the heavenly vision*" (Acts xxvi. 19). If Paul was a great companion of Jesus Christ, it was because he had completely finished with everything but Jesus Christ. He says: "*I count all things but loss for the excellency of the knowledge of Christ Jesus my Lord*" (Philippians iii. 8—A.V.). He was a man who was wholly on the ground of Jesus Christ, and wholly on the ground of God's heavenly purpose. Such are the companions of Jesus Christ.

There are many young Christians here and perhaps you do not know your Bible as well as some older Christians do, and you do not know all the Bible background of what I have been saying. I hope this will make you want to know your Bible better! But perhaps there is a lot

that I have said that you do not understand. Now this is
one thing that I do want you to understand—you will
come to understand all the other as you go on, if you hold
fast your beginning firm unto the end. If you really do
commit yourself to the Lord Jesus you will come to
understand. But that is not what I was going to say: what
I was going to say is this:

What I want you to realize is that you have a very
much greater Christ than you have ever imagined. The
Christ to whom you have given yourselves is a very
great Christ. The call of the Lord which you have
answered in accepting the Lord Jesus is a much bigger
calling than you have any knowledge of. I just want you
to go away with this impression: 'My, I have come into
something! This is big enough to fill my whole life.'

So don't worry about what you do not understand, but
do realize how great a Lord is your Lord, and what a
great thing is the heavenly calling.

CHAPTER THREE

THE LORD'S TABLE AND THE COMPANIONS

Reading: Exodus xii. 1-16, 21-24.
Luke xxii. 1, 7, 8, 14-21.

WE HAVE BEEN seeing something of what the Lord is seeking in the way of companions of a heavenly calling. We have also been seeing how the Israel of old failed Him in that respect and how, in the time of their final failure, He revealed what He had ever had in His heart, even before there was an Israel—that is, a people of a heavenly life and a spiritual nature.

The Lord's Table is perhaps the most beautiful expression of this wonderful reality of companionship with Christ.

Judas had gone out. He had taken sides with the rejecting Israel and was numbered with them in judgment, so it was not only one man but a whole nation that went out that night. Judas was but the representative of the nation which rejected Christ and was rejected by God. It is impressive that such a representative of the rejecting Israel should be right there in the presence of the companions of Christ! And there, in the inner circle, he demonstrated what had become true of Israel—he was no companion of Christ.

So, with the rejecting Israel gone out, the companions were left with their Master. Of them He was able to say: *"Ye are they which have continued with me in my temptations"* (Luke xxii. 28).

This Lord's Table, or Lord's Supper, is one of the great features of the transition from the old Israel to the new heavenly, spiritual Israel. What the Passover was intended to mean in the old Israel has become true in the new Israel. We are, therefore, going to look at some of the features of the Passover which relate to the companions of Jesus.

We go back to the twelfth chapter of the Book of Exodus, where the Passover was first instituted and established, and look right into the heart of this matter to see exactly what it did mean. When we have looked closely enough we discover this; that it was the great contest between God and the gods of Egypt. God summed it all up when He said that that night He was going to finish and complete His judgment not only upon the Egyptians but upon all the gods of the Egyptians. The nine judgments which had preceded had been declared to be against the gods of the Egyptians, and you do not understand those plagues unless you recognize that factor. If it were necessary we could show you how each judgment had some relationship to the gods of Egypt. Just as an example: the frog was a sacred thing in Egypt. It was worshipped as representing a god, and God— Jehovah—turned their very gods upon themselves in judgment. So it was with every judgment. They worshipped the sun, so God blotted it out.

The whole thing is being gathered up and consummated on this Passover night. God is going to finish this quarrel that He had with the Egyptians because of their gods. He is a very jealous God and He had said: "*Thou shalt have none other gods before me*" (Exodus xx. 3).

That is the heart of the thing, and we must carry that over to the Lord's Table. In the first place this Table means: No compromise with anything that is against God. It is to be the Lord, and the Lord alone.

The second thing to be noted is the focal point of this whole settlement—the first-born sons of all in Egypt. In those days, and even today, the first-born is representative of all the others. He includes the whole family, and if you touch the first-born, you are touching the parents and the family. So all the Egyptians were represented in their first-born—and the Lord said "*I . . . will smite all the first-born in the land of Egypt, both man and beast*". Another kind of first-born, which was not of God, had to be set aside in order to bring in what the Letter to the Hebrews calls the "*church of the first-born*" (Hebrews xii. 23). One first-born must be removed to make room for the other first-born.

Those who rightly partake at the Table are of the "*church of the first-born*". They are those who have been born again by the Spirit of God, and they are the companions of Christ.

Then note the third thing: the point where this whole thing was settled. It was all settled on the threshold of every home. It is a pity that the translators have not been consistent in translating a Hebrew word which you read twice in Exodus xii. 22: "*Ye shall take a bunch of hyssop, and dip it in the blood that is in the bason, and strike the lintel and the two side posts with the blood that is in the bason*". Evidently the translators could not get the idea of the Hebrew there and so they used the word 'basin', as that seemed to suit it best. Of course, in their minds the blood would be collected into a basin, and so the bunch of hyssop would be dipped into the basin. But the Hebrew word 'saph' is translated 'threshold' elsewhere in the Old Testament. What ought to have been said was: 'You shall take a bunch of hyssop and dip it into the blood that is on the threshold.' You probably know that the threshold of a house is its most sacred place. You are very particular

C

about who crosses the threshold into your house, and that is why some superstitious people put charms over it. Sometimes it is a horseshoe—something to keep evil away, or, as they call it, 'bad luck'.

This thing has become a superstition, but behind it is this great spiritual truth—there is a threshold that God looks at as being very sacred, and behind that threshold where the blood is are His own companions. The threshold signifies a division between His companions and His enemies. Did you notice that Moses said: *"None of you shall go out of the door of his house until the morning"*? In effect he said 'Don't let any man cross that threshold into the realm where the enemies are. Let that blood-sprinkled threshold become a division between you, the Lord's own companions, and those He is going to judge.' Judas went out over the threshold when it was night.

I believe that even today (certainly it was so up to recent times) in the Jewish ritual of the Passover there is a point where the first-born goes out and opens the outside door, the door by the threshold. Then he comes back and places an empty chair at the table and an extra cup on the table. That is done in the hope that the Lord's messenger will cross the threshold, come in and take part with them. That is not here in the Bible, of course, but the Hebrews knew the meaning of the threshold—something sacred to the Lord, an open door to the Lord.

Judas went out across the threshold and he met the judgment of this world. The companions of Jesus stayed inside that night. They were protected by the precious blood and were saved from death.

The picture behind Exodus xii is of the rightful Lord coming to His world to claim His rights, and He says: 'This is the sign and the token. Whether you own Me as your rightful Lord, or whether you do not, the sign is the sprinkled blood. When I see the blood I know that you are My friends and that you are loyal to Me. If I do not see the blood I know that you are enemies, and you will meet My judgment. My executioner is with Me and when I see the blood I say "Not in there. Leave them alone. They are My friends." When I do not see the blood I say "You go in there".' You notice that the Lord speaks in this chapter as though He is one person, and the one who is going to give judgment is another. He sends someone in. That is the picture behind the Passover.

There is just one other thing that we will mention. It is not said here in this chapter of Exodus, but it is definitely said in other places. Jeremiah (in chapter xxxi) says that on the night of the Passover the Lord took Israel by the hand and betrothed her to Himself. In principle, then, the Passover was a marriage ceremony. To use the language of the prophets, the Lord that night took the virgin of Israel and betrothed her unto Himself, and He made a blood covenant with her. What a lot that opens up as to the marriage relationship! It is a relationship with blood— *"they shall be one flesh"* (Genesis ii. 24). If ever Israel had anything to do with other gods from that time it was called whoredom, fornication, adultery. It was a breach of the marriage covenant.

That is why Israel was eventually abandoned by God. They remained very religious, and still kept up the ceremony of the Passover—but the Lord Jesus said: *"Ye are of your father the devil, and the lusts of your father it is your will to do"* (John viii. 44). It was the devil's work to bring Jesus Christ to crucifixion, and Israel was the devil's instrument in doing it. It was the last phase of a long history of rejecting the Lord and breaking the marriage covenant.

That is the dark side. Let us look on the bright side!

The Lord Jesus, in constituting the new heavenly Israel on the principles of the old, took up this very thing, in all these respects, and in this one, I think, in particular. There was a marriage supper that night in the upper room. Jesus betrothed His Church unto Himself in a covenant of blood—"*This cup is the new covenant in my blood*"—and so He secured His companions of the heavenly calling. Later we shall speak more fully of the 'Bride'.

We must apply all this to ourselves. On the one side it is very searching. It says: 'No compromise with anything whatever that is against the Lord.' I wonder if, every time there is a service of Holy Communion, people recognize that that is the meaning—a real and utter division between companions of the Lord and others! In the Lord's Table we celebrate our betrothal. We were joined to the Lord in holy matrimony—by His precious blood made His Bride. The marriage of the Lamb is the *great* coming event (Revelation xix 7).

CHAPTER FOUR

THE TRUE BASIS OF LIFE FOR THE COMPANIONS

AT THIS TIME I want to try and help young Christians in relation to two words which are the great words of the Christian life: 'heavenly' and 'faith'. You will have noticed, if you know the Letter to the Hebrews at all, that these are two of the most prominent words in it.

This word 'heavenly', in its different forms, occurs quite a number of times in this Letter:

"Wherefore, holy brethren, companions of a heavenly calling" (Hebrews iii. 1).

"Having then a great high priest, who hath passed through the heavens, Jesus the Son of God" (Hebrews iv. 14).

"For as touching those who were once enlightened and tasted of the heavenly gift" (Hebrews vi. 4).

"Now in the things which we are saying the chief point is this: We have such a high priest, who sat down on the throne of the Majesty in the heavens" (Hebrews viii. 1).

"Who serve that which is a copy and shadow of the heavenly things" (Hebrews viii. 5).

"It was necessary therefore that the copies of the things in the heavens should be cleansed with these: but the heavenly things themselves with better sacrifices than these" (Hebrews ix. 23).

"But now they desire a better country, that is, a heavenly" (Hebrews xi. 16).

"*To the general assembly and church of the first-born who are enrolled in heaven, and to God the Judge of all, and to the spirits of just men made perfect*" (Hebrews xii. 23).

"*Whose voice then shook the earth: but now he hath promised, saying, Yet once more will I make to tremble not the earth only, but also the heaven*" (Hebrews xii. 26).

So, you see, the Letter has a lot to say about heavenly things, and here, in chapter three, it says that we are called in relation to these heavenly things. Our calling is a heavenly calling, unto a heavenly life: not after this life, but *now*.

I am not going to cite all the occurrences of the word 'faith'! It has a very large place in this Letter, and, as you know, one whole chapter is given up to faith—chapter eleven.

Here are these two words: 'heavenly' and 'faith', and they are very difficult words for young Christians to understand. If we say to young Christians: 'Now you are called to a life of faith', they may think of that in a very limited way: that they have to believe God, that God is able to save, that God is able to keep, that God is able to provide. That is all true, but we are going to see that it means much more than that. If we say to a young Christian: 'You are called now to live a heavenly life', I do not know what he or she would think! What a difficult idea that is! They would probably say: 'Well, how can we live a heavenly life when we have to live down here on this earth?'

Well, let us try to help such people, and everybody else. Let me say again that 'heavenly' and 'faith' are one thing.

We are going right back to the Old Testament for illustration, and I am going to use another big word. When God took up an instrument, in the form of a person or a people, He always put that instrument, that person, or that people, on a super-natural basis. He took every measure to see that the basis of their life was a super-natural one. He took them completely off a natural basis, and for them, if there was not the super-natural, there was nothing at all. They found it difficult, but it was in that way that they learned that they had come into relation with a super-natural God, a God who was altogether above the natural. So God created naturally impossible situations for these people and then, in solving the problem of the naturally impossible, He showed them what a great Lord He was.

Let us look at some illustrations. We will begin with Abraham—and he has a large place in this Letter to the Hebrews. Abraham was chosen by God for a very great purpose. We shall see more about that later, but let us be content with the simple statement of fact for the present. Abraham was called to be the father of a race which God was going to raise up and through which His Son, Jesus Christ, would come. God said to him: "*In thy seed shall all the nations of the earth be blessed*" (Genesis xxii. 18). Notice: 'In *thy* seed'—and then God went away and left him and did nothing more about it for a long time. God came back and repeated His promise, but by then Abraham was ninety years old and his wife was nearly as old—and yet God was saying: 'In *thy* seed'. An utterly impossible situation naturally! 'Impossible!' said Sarah, 'Altogether out of the question! We must do something about this.' And you know what they did. They tried to do God's work on natural lines. Sarah sent for her handmaid, Hagar, and they tried to fulfil God's promise in that natural way. But those of us who know our Bibles know quite well that that was not God's way, and He was having none of it. God kept to His own ground—

super-natural ground. If this thing was ever to be, only
God all-mighty could do it. No man nor woman could
do it, and neither could both of them together. Only God
could do it—and He did it! He put them on to super-
natural ground. It was a big test of faith! It was not
earthly ground, but heavenly ground. It was not natural
ground, but the ground of faith. And that is how God
did it.

That is our first illustration, and that runs right
through the Bible.

We pass from Abraham and Isaac to Jacob. Jacob came
into the birthright. He was intended by God to have it—
that is, he was intended to be the next link in God's
chain, the next step of God in the onward march of His
eternal purpose, but Jacob took the thing into his own
hands. In effect he said: 'I am going to do this.' So he
deceived his parent and robbed his brother . . . but his
whole little plan broke down. He had to leave home and
go many miles away to his uncle, and for twenty years
there was no sign of God going on with His purpose.
When you come on to Jacob at the end of that time you
find a very disillusioned man and a man who is very much
afraid of what is going to happen to him. He is making
plans for his own safety when he meets with his brother—
and then God meets him. You know the story of that
night when God met Jacob! Jacob had tried to realize
God's intention on natural grounds, and God entirely
destroyed those grounds. In that night Jacob came clearly
to understand that if God was going to fulfil any purpose
in his life, only He could do it. When God changed his
name from Jacob to Israel He changed the man from the
earthly to the heavenly, from the natural man to the
man of faith, and then God went on with him. God could
never go on with Jacob while he was resting upon his own

natural ground. When God got him off that ground on to heavenly ground, then they could go on together.

We pass from Jacob to Joseph. The story of Joseph is one of the most fascinating stories of the Old Testament! A lot of unkind things have been said about Joseph when he was a young man. Of course, it is usually the old people who do that! Joseph had some dreams, and, well, young men are allowed to have dreams! You perhaps remember the dreams: he dreamt that sun, moon and stars were bowing down to him, and other things were doing the same. Perhaps he did make a mistake when he told his dreams to his brothers. They were shrewd enough to see the point, and they interpreted the dreams as against themselves. They said: 'Are we going to bow down to you? You are our young brother. We will never bow down to you!'

Now, you can say what you like about Joseph's indiscretion, but those dreams became literally true. The day came when his brothers were cringing before him, trembling for their very lives. 'Oh, sir,' they said, 'have mercy upon us!' Those dreams became true. There was something of God in that, and I think that Joseph always had those dreams in his heart.

Joseph was going to come, in the will of God, to a high place, and to serve God in a great piece of work. It was no less than preserving alive the whole of God's chosen nation.

However, these brothers—well, they had a conference, and the point of their discussion was how they could get rid of this young brother of theirs. One of the brothers said: 'Let us kill him, and we will soak his coat in his own blood, send it back to our father and say that a wild beast has destroyed him.' Another brother said: 'No, don't let's kill him. Let us put him into a pit.' So they put

him into a deep pit. It was just another way of killing
him—to let him die there. They left him and went off.
Then they saw some camels coming and a caravan passing
across where they were. So they decided to take Joseph
out of the pit and sell him. Accordingly they sold him to
these traders, who were going down to Egypt, and he
was taken and sold in Egypt as a slave. Oh, wonderful
sovereignty of God! Joseph had just *got* to get down to
Egypt! God had ordained that he should go, for it was
there that he was to do his great work of saving his
nation. But Joseph never thought of that way of getting
to Egypt!

However, he got there, and became the slave of a great
man. We will not fill in all the details, but by the treachery
of that man's wife, Joseph was put into a dungeon and
was left there for years. Where were his dreams now?
The whole situation was quite impossible—but God had
made it so. This whole purpose could never be realized
on natural grounds. It could only be realized on super-
natural ground—and if ever a man was put on super-
natural ground, that man was Joseph! But this transition
from the earthly to the heavenly, from the natural to the
life of faith, was a difficult passage. It was very hard on
the flesh—and it always is! But the super-natural Lord
did it. No one could ever say that Joseph did it, or put it
down to a man. Only God could do it. It was on super-
natural ground, on heavenly ground, not earthly. It was
the way of faith and not of sight.

I suppose I ought to put in a very large section here on
Israel. That nation, saved through Joseph, was after
many years found in slavery itself in Egypt. God had said
to Abraham that they would be in Egypt as slaves for four
hundred years, but that they would come out of that
slavery. He would bring them out by a mighty hand.

However, they were here in Egypt and things were going from bad to worse, and from worse to awful. The whole situation was as hopeless as it could be, and to make it as impossible as could be, Pharaoh decided to kill all the little boys that were born at that time. I need not tell you the rest of the story! "*At that season*", it says, "*Moses was born*" (Acts vii. 20). Moses was born at that impossible time, and will you tell me that it was not a super-natural thing that he was preserved alive when all the boys were being massacred? It was on super-natural ground, not natural, on heavenly ground, not earthly. We only need just to pass our eye over the account of the deliverance of the people of Israel from Egypt—what we call the 'Exodus'—and, my, what a difficult situation it was! Pharaoh had employed all his resources to prevent those people from going out. There was nothing he had not used to make the exodus impossible, but God stepped in when the situation was at its darkest and brought them out with a strong hand, as He had said He would all those years before. The exodus was on super-natural ground.

The story of the forty years in the wilderness is the same. If you do not believe it was super-natural, go and try living in a wilderness for forty years! Go especially to that wilderness! I have passed over it a number of times in an aeroplane and I have said: 'How on earth could a nation live in this for forty years?' The answer was: they did not 'on earth' at all. They did it from heaven. God fed them and protected them from heaven. In every way it was a heavenly life. It was not natural: it was God. He had put that nation on to a super-natural basis.

We come to the end of that time and go on to Joshua. We know what he had to face! There were all those

strong and very wicked nations in the land of Canaan,
and Joshua had got to lead the people in, take possession
of the land and drive out all those nations. Do you think
that could have been done naturally? No, God took
over and the people of Israel went in. They crossed the
Jordan when it was overflowing all its banks, and they
went over with dry feet. The rest of the story is known
to you.

We pass on many years and come to the book of
Judges. We will just take one illustration from that book.
Israel was now being beset by other very strong nations
and the time came when the Midianites, as many *"as the
sand which is upon the sea shore for multitude"* (Judges vii.
12), gathered around Israel. The situation was anything
but easy! The Lord called Gideon and told him that he
was to go out against this combination of armies and
that he would deliver Israel from them. Gideon said:
'This wants a big army', so he sent out to all Israel and
got a very big army together—at least, it was what was
called a big army then. He had twenty-two thousand
men. But the Lord said to Gideon: 'You have too big an
army. It is quite true that all these other enemies are
many, many times more than your army, but your army
is too big.' So Gideon put a test to them, and a great
multitude went home and left him with a much smaller
army. And the Lord said: 'They are still too many.'
Surely He is moving Gideon on to heavenly ground!
When God had finished with Gideon he had just three
hundred men, and He said: *"By the three hundred men . . .
will I save you"* (Judges vii. 7)—and He did it.

Notice how He put Gideon on to heavenly, super-
natural ground. It was a very testing thing for Gideon!
Do you tell me that that was not faith? Faith and the
heavenly go together.

Are you beginning to see the meaning of what is heavenly and what is faith? Faith is, that heaven can do what no man or men can do. Nothing is impossible to heaven in any circumstances or situation.

Well, that is not all. You remember that later Israel went into captivity in Babylon, and they were there for seventy years. At the end of that time they were in a very poor state, but when it was put to them that the time had come for them to return to their country the great majority said: 'No, it is impossible. It is no use going back there. The whole situation is hopeless. The land is in desolation and the city is destroyed. We have not got the heart for it.' But a remnant returned, and you know the details of how God came in for them in a sovereign way. He provided for them all that they needed and helped them in marvellous ways, so that they rebuilt the city and their temple and made their land productive again. But it was a super-natural thing. The majority vote was 'Impossible!' The minority believed God.

Where shall we stop? Let us leave the Old Testament and come to Him to whom all this was pointing—Jesus. It was all leading on to Him. God had promised to send His Son. The prophets were just full of the coming of the Messiah, but the ideas about the Messiah on the part of Israel were very natural ones: 'Of course, he will be a great ruler, a man with tremendous power. Everyone will gather to him. He will set up this wonderful kingdom of Israel and the Romans will be thrown out of our country.' That was their natural idea of their Messiah— but when He came there was no room for Him at His birth, and the ruling authority of that time started the old game of killing all the little boys, with the special object of getting his hands upon this one boy. The very

survival of Jesus was a heavenly miracle! His birth was a
heavenly thing, a super-natural thing, and the same was
true of His life. How many times do we read: 'They took
counsel that they might kill Him', and 'They took up
stones to stone Him'? His fulfilling of His ministry was
a heavenly thing. It was super-natural.

And what about His death? They took counsel to kill
Him and decided they were going to do it. Then they
said: 'We won't do it at the Passover. That will be the
wrong time' . . . and God said: 'I have this matter in
hand. It will be My matter and not yours. It will be on
exactly the day that I choose, and that will be the day of
the Passover.' Jesus said about His dying: "*No man taketh
it (My life) away from me, but I lay it down of myself. I have
power to lay it down and I have power to take it again. This
commandment received I from my Father*" (John x. 18). He
was saying that when it happened it would not be in
man's hands, it would be in God's hands. And in spite
of their decisions and their counsels, it *was* on the
day of the Passover! It had to be. Many, many generations were involved in that. The death and resurrection
of Jesus Christ were super-natural—not of man, but
of God.

I could go on from that to the Church. The whole
history of the Church, from its beginning on the Day of
Pentecost, is a miracle. It was persecuted in its early years
and there were many massacres of Christians. The Roman
Empire decided that Christianity must be wiped out
from the earth, and at that time, and many times since,
the Church has passed through very, very serious crises.
But the Church of God marches on! It is still here and
it is still growing. It is super-natural.

Now, why all this? This is not something which is
peculiar to Abraham, Moses, Joshua and Gideon. It is

not something which is limited to these men of the Old Testament. This Letter to the Hebrews is written to Christians. It is written for us, and it says that we are *"holy brethren, companions of a heavenly calling"*. We are the companions of Christ, but God has put us on the same basis as that on which He always did put His people.

The older Christians know quite well from experience what I am talking about. How often in our history have situations arisen—not that we have brought about—which were quite impossible! We say: 'God allowed them.' Perhaps we ought to say: 'God appointed them.' God has put our lives on this basis. Our salvation is a super-natural thing or it is nothing! Poor Nicodemus, the man who could not see further than nature, with all his intelligence, said: *"How can a man be born when he is old?"* (John iii. 4). Our new birth is a miracle, our sustenance in the Christian life, that is, being able to keep going, is a miracle; and our survival and our triumph in many and many an impossible situation are super-natural. And at last our translation to glory will be super-natural. You may die naturally, but you will not naturally rise again. That will be God's doing. And if it is going to be true that we share His glory, we, who know ourselves, would gladly say: 'That will be a miracle! A creature such as I am sharing the glory of Jesus Christ for all eternity! My, that will be super-natural!'

This is the meaning of faith—just that you believe that heaven can do what no one else can do. Faith is a very practical thing. A whole situation is naturally hopeless. What are we going to do about it? Are we going to give it all up and say: 'It is impossible. This is the end of everything. We are finished'? Or are we going to say: 'Yes, it is like that naturally, but God . . . but heaven . . .'

Heaven is greater than earth and God is greater than all.

That is the message of this Letter to the Hebrews. I hope you understand a little better what it means to live a heavenly life. It is living on the resources that heaven has for us when all other resources have gone.

CHAPTER FIVE

THE CHANGED POSITION OF THE COMPANIONS

As A SUBJECT, we have pointed out that this is a key to the whole of this Letter to the Hebrews, which is an appeal for companions of Christ, and for companions of a heavenly calling. We have also said that this Letter is a summary of the whole of the New Testament. In making that statement, of course, we provide you with a very large field of consideration. We simply have to say that all that is in the New Testament is gathered in some way into this Letter. Therefore, all that is in the New Testament is gathered up into this one thought: God is seeking companions for His Son in a heavenly calling.

We are now going to dig more deeply into this Letter, always with this one thought in mind: It is companions of Christ which are in view.

Let us say one brief word about the point of view taken by this Letter. We understand that it was written and given to these Hebrew Christians at a time of very serious crisis, when a whole system which had existed for many centuries was about to pass away. The whole system of the Old Testament, from Moses onward, was about to go. After the writer had put down all that is in this Letter he put over it a quotation from the Old Testament: *"Yet once more will I make to tremble not the earth only, but also the heaven. And this word, Yet once more, signifieth the removing of those things that are shaken, as of things that have been made, that those things which are not shaken may remain"* (Hebrews xii. 26, 27—quoted from Haggai ii. 6). By quoting that Scripture and putting it at the end of this Letter, the writer indicated that this was just about to take place, and he proved to be right. It is evident that this Letter was written just before A.D. 70.

The Roman legions may already have been gathering around Jerusalem, and we know from history what happened. The city was besieged and destroyed, not one stone of the temple being left standing upon another, and the whole land was desolated. The priestly service ceased and all the functions of the temple came to an end. The whole country was put into a state of utter desolation, and from that day, even until now, that system ceased to be.

And this Letter was written because the Lord knew what was going to happen and because, in the Divine plan, the time had come for it to happen. Always read this Letter in the light of that great historic crisis.

That was the dark side of the story. But you will notice that this Letter is just full of that 'better thing' which had taken the place of the old, and we shall be dwelling upon that 'better thing' as we go along. As the people of an earthly calling were being set aside this great Letter of a heavenly calling was presented to them.

Before we go further with the Letter, let us remember that its message abides for us. It would be a very blind person who today could not see that another such event is very near. There has been built up on this earth another great system of Christianity. It is very earthly as a system, and, just as the hearts of the Jews here were very much bound up with their system, so in our time multitudes of Christians are just bound up with this historic Christian-

ity. I do not claim to be a prophet, but there is much
in the Word of God which points to the time when this
whole system will be shaken. It is very impressive that in
our lifetime we have seen this in a small way, when
churches have been destroyed, congregations scattered,
and it has not been possible to go on with the old forms.
People have had to find the Lord for themselves without
any earthly helps. They have had to get their help from
heaven and not from earth. We have seen this happen,
in a comparatively small way, on at least two occasions.
The Lord has smitten the earth on two terrible occasions,
with not so many years between them, and it is not
difficult to see that it could happen again on a very much
bigger scale. That event may not be very far off. We
Christians speak of the coming of the Lord. That is our
hope and our salvation: but we must remember that the
coming of the Lord is going to be accompanied by a
terrible judgment upon this earth, when everything that
is not heavenly is going to be shaken, so shaken that it
will just collapse.

So this Letter has a real message for us. As was said to
the Jewish Christians at that time: 'Your whole system,
in which you are so bound up, is going to pass away', so
this Letter says to us today: 'All the earthly system is
going to be shaken, and shaken out of its place. But there
is a better one coming'—"*God having provided some better
thing*" (Hebrews xi. 40).

Well, that is the standpoint of this Letter. I am sure we
can see that it is very applicable to our time. We are not
just studying a book of the Bible which relates to many
centuries ago. God is the eternal God and He speaks to
all time, but the message is intensified as we get nearer
the end.

Now we are going to see further this transition from

the earthly to the heavenly. In the terms of the New Testament, and of this Letter in particular, it is the transition from an earthly, historic Israel to a heavenly, spiritual Israel. So we are going to look at the beginnings of Israel in both cases.

Do you notice how the Letter begins? It begins with one word: 'God'. You can put a big ring round that word. God stands over the whole content of this Letter. Everything in it must be viewed from God's standpoint, not from man's, or from the world's, or from the earthly standpoint. It is God who is speaking, and all that is here is what God is saying. God stands over all that this Letter contains, and no one is allowed to say that this thing is of man. As we move through the Letter we have constantly to say to ourselves: 'God is saying that. This is not the interpretation of man. This is God speaking.' The great transition which is marked by this Letter is God moving forward. God is going on. God is in charge of everything. And the Letter says: 'The companions of the heavenly way are those who are moving on with God.' The appeal of the Letter is: 'Let us go on, because God is going on.'

The whole of the old Jewish system was something which had settled down, and in a very real sense it had gone to sleep. God is not the God of the spiritually asleep. The appeal to Israel was: 'Awake, thou that sleepest!' That system had gone to sleep, had settled down and had become an end in itself. It was not moving on with God. That was the trouble in the days of the prophets. And this Letter says: 'God is going on. The companions of Christ are those who are going on with God.'

Do remember this: that a true, living Christianity is a 'going on' Christianity. It will never stop going on, in this life or in eternity. It says: "*Of his government . . . there shall be no end*" (Isaiah ix. 7). So we begin with God, and we move on with God.

This Letter is God expressing Himself. That is in the very first statement in the Letter: "*God, having of old time spoken unto the fathers in the prophets by divers portions and in divers manners, hath at the end of these days spoken unto us in his Son*". Here, then, we meet with a God who is expressing Himself. He is here declared to be a speaking God; He is not a dumb or silent God. He is a God who has always been speaking and is speaking now. So, right at the beginning, this Letter declares God to be a God who speaks. And then, to analyse it further, He is spoken of as being a God who speaks with a purpose. He is a God of purpose and is speaking concerning His purpose. He spoke in times past "*in the prophets by divers portions*". He speaks now in His Son, and here there are two very important things to note.

In times past God spoke in many parts, by many prophets. He said one thing through one prophet and another thing through a different prophet. All the prophets were parts of God's speaking. No one prophet said everything. You can look into the prophets and see that every one of them had a specific aspect of God's message. "In many parts", is the word. His final speech in Christ is the gathering up of all the parts into completeness. God's Son is the complete speech of God—all the parts are brought together in Him. That gives this Letter a very, very big place, does it not? It says that now, here, God is speaking in fulness in His Son.

And alongside of that is the appeal "*to give the more earnest heed*" (Hebrews ii. 1), because this is so much fuller than anything that God had ever said before.

Then it says that in times past God spoke 'in many

ways', not only in different portions, but in different manners. It would take too long for us to go back to the Old Testament to see all the manners in which God spoke. He spoke by a thousand different means: sometimes by words and sometimes by acts. The manners were indeed 'divers'. However, the statement here is that at the end He speaks in one way, one all-inclusive way, and that is in His Son. God's Son is His one inclusive way of speaking at the end. On the one side, no one is going to get anything from God apart from Jesus Christ. God will absolutely refuse to speak other than in His Son. If you want to know what God wants to say to you, you have to come to His Son. On the other side, in Jesus Christ we have all that God ever wants to say.

I want to say that especially to young Christians. I have been reading and studying my Bible all through the years, and I tell you quite honestly that today this book is altogether beyond me. I would never come back to this Letter to the Hebrews if that were not true. I have preached and lectured on this Letter for years, but today it is far beyond me. Should I say 'the Letter to the Hebrews'? I would be more correct in saying 'the Lord Jesus who is revealed in this Letter'.

Yes, we have far more of God's speaking in His Son than we have yet come to understand. We have nothing apart from Jesus Christ, and we *need* nothing apart from Him.

We said that this letter presents God as a God of purpose, and it goes on to show that His purpose is centred and summed up in His Son. That is set before us at the beginning of the Letter in three ways.

Firstly, in the person of His Son. Just look at this: "*At the end of these days (He hath) spoken unto us in his Son, whom he appointed heir of all things, through whom also he made the worlds; who being the effulgence of his glory, and the very image of his substance. . . ."* You notice that the whole of the first chapter is occupied with presenting God's Son. God is speaking concerning His Son, as to who He is. What a great Son this is!

Then it presents the Son in terms of redemption. *"He made purification of sins".* That is just one phrase, but many chapters follow to explain what that redemption is. All these chapters on priesthood and sacrifice have to do with that one clause. God is speaking in His Son concerning redemption.

In the third place He is speaking in His Son concerning glory. The Son is *"the effulgence of his glory"*, and He is going to bring *"many sons unto glory"* (Hebrews ii. 10), because *"when he had made purification of sins, (He) sat down on the right hand of the Majesty on high".* God speaks in a Son whom He has now glorified and sat at His own right hand.

But God does not speak in His Son and leave it there. You will notice that in chapter two He brings man into this, and this Letter has a wonderful message for man: that all that God has put in His Son is for man. God speaks in this Letter of the finished work of Christ, the work which is made complete *for man.*

Here is something that you and I must dwell upon. Personally, I am constantly brought to this: I have not yet learnt thoroughly to believe what I believe in! I believe in the finished work of Christ, yet sometimes I am just as miserable about myself as any man could be. I am often almost at the point of giving up because of what a wretched kind of thing I am. If there is anything in this world that would cause me to give up the Christian ministry, it is myself. Do you understand what I mean? Oh, how we are discouraged by what we find in our-

selves! And so, we don't believe what we believe in. We
believe in the finished work of Christ, and that God puts
all that finished work to our account. God does not see
us in ourselves—He sees us in Christ. He does not see us,
He sees Christ in us. We don't believe that! If we really
did we would be delivered from ourselves and would
indeed be triumphant Christians.

Of course, that does not mean that we can just behave
anyhow. We may speak and act wrongly, but for every
Christian there is a refuge—a mercy-seat. It has not to be
made; it *is* there with the precious Blood. That has not
to be shed; it *is* shed. There is a High Priest making intercession for us. There is everything that we need. The
work is finished, completed. Oh, we Christians must
believe our beliefs! We must take hold, with both hands,
of the things which are of our Christian faith.

But I know you have problems when I say that:
'What about this old man?' Perhaps you are one of those
people who believe that sin has been absolutely rooted
out of you and that it is quite impossible for you to sin—
well, if you believe that, the Lord bless you! I think you
may be tripped up one day and find that there is an old
man there after all. But leaving that aside, most of us do
know that there are two things in us—there is the new
and there is the old, there is the spiritual man and there is
the natural man, and this natural man is a very trouble-
some fellow! What about him over against the finished
work? This Letter tells you all about that when it says:
"*God dealeth with you as with sons*" (xii. 7), and God loves
sons. Are you a child of God? Has there been in your
history that deep action of new birth? Have you received
the Lord Jesus? The Word of God says: "*As many as
received him, to them gave he the right to become children of
God*" (John i. 12). If you have received the Lord Jesus you

are a child of God. The spirit of sonship has come in and dwells in you.

This Letter says that God loves His sons, and therefore He chastens them: He child-trains them, and 'no child-training', says the Letter, 'for the present is pleasant'. God's dealings with His own family are not always pleasant, and when they are unpleasant there is a little demon sitting on our shoulder who will whisper in our ear: 'You see, God does not love you. He would not deal with you like this if He loved you.' The devil is always out to turn the loving works of God into evil things.

Yes, God is dealing with us as with sons. It is discipline, and it goes against the flesh. The Letter says: 'It is not for the present pleasant.' Indeed, it might have said: 'It is very unpleasant!' 'What father is he', says this Letter, 'who does not chasten his son?'

What I am saying is not easy to say, because I may be exposing myself to the rod. We have enough experience to know that we have to say some things very carefully, because we are often tested on the things that we say. But here is the statement that it is a totally unkind father who never chastens his child. Have you seen children who are never chastened or corrected? Those children are going to have a bad time in this world, as people are not going to like them, and they will discover that. Their parents have spoilt them.

This Letter says that God's love is expressed in His using the rod to His children. He does not always put His good things, His best things, into a nice form. I heard the other day of a little boy who had to take some medicine, and it was not very nice. His father said: 'There are many vitamins in this medicine.' The little boy said: 'Daddy, why must all the good things be put into nasty

things? Why can't they be put into ice-cream?' The
Lord does not always put the good things into ice-cream.
Sometimes the vitamins are in the nasty medicine.

Now that is exactly what this Letter says. God is not
condemning us when He deals with us like that. He is
working to deliver us. If you think that these talks here
are going to save you, you are making a mistake! They
are only to explain what God is doing. God never saves
by theory. You can read everything that has ever been
written on Christian doctrine and still be the same man
or woman. God's ways are very practical, and He
teaches us by experience. That experience is sometimes very difficult and is called here 'the training of
sons'.

May the Lord Jesus just impress our hearts again with
these things! God is still speaking in His Son, and His
speaking is in order to get companions of His Son.
Companions of this heavenly calling and of Christ will
go into the hard school and have to learn many hard
lessons, but in learning them they will come to
understand how great is their inheritance in the Lord
Jesus.

I may add this: My experience is that no one really has
spiritual knowledge without suffering. I am not speaking
about head knowledge. I am speaking about real knowledge of the Lord in the inner life. I do not know of
anyone who has come into that knowledge apart from
suffering. Perhaps that is a depressing thing to say, but
there it is—it is a law in God's Word. "*We have this
treasure in earthen vessels*" (II Corinthians iv. 7), and how
poor this vessel is we learn through trial and affliction,
but then we learn how wonderful the Lord is. The Letter
to the Hebrews says: "*Afterward*" (that is, after the
chastening) "*the peaceable fruit of righteousness*" (xii. 11).

What a wonderful phrase! Those fruits come along the line of chastening and by way of suffering.

So let us ask for that grace which the Apostle had to rejoice in suffering.

CHAPTER SIX

SOME TITLES AS EVIDENCE OF THE CHANGE

THE POINT AT which we have now arrived is that, in the constituting of the spiritual Israel, God is following the same line as He took with the earthly Israel, but with one great difference—with the earthly He followed temporal lines, but with the heavenly He is following spiritual lines. However, they are both one in principle. We have seen something of this and are now going to see a little more.

Surely it must be perfectly true that this is what God is doing. The Letter to the Hebrews is the great document of the transition from one Israel to another, and in it there are many evidences of this truth. If anyone has any doubt at all, there is one fragment which should settle all such questions:

"For ye are not come unto a mount that might be touched, and that burned with fire, and unto blackness, and darkness, and tempest, and the sound of a trumpet, and the voice of words; which voice they that heard intreated that no word should be spoken unto them: for they could not endure that which was enjoined. If even a beast touch the mountain, it shall be stoned; and so fearful was the appearance, that Moses said, I exceedingly fear and quake" (Hebrews xii. 18-21).

That is the old Israel being constituted at the mount. However, the word to us is: 'Ye are not come to that. That is not God's way of constituting His new Israel.'

"But ye are come unto mount Zion, and unto the city of the living God, the heavenly Jerusalem, and to innumerable hosts of angels, to the general assembly and church of the first-born who are enrolled in heaven, and to God the Judge of all, and to the spirits of just men made perfect, and to Jesus the mediator of a new covenant, and to the blood of sprinkling that speaketh better than that of Abel" (Hebrews xii. 22-24).

That surely settles all argument! If we had only that paragraph in the New Testament we should know the difference between the old dispensation and the new, between Judaism and Christianity, and between what *they* were in and what *we* are in.

But that is not all: it is only a part of the whole argument. I would have you note some of the titles in this Letter which are evidences of this truth:

(i) *God's family*

We all know that God looked upon Israel as His family. He said to Pharaoh: *"Let my son go"* (Exodus iv. 22). The evidence is too much for us to follow through, but it is quite clear that Israel of old was, in a certain sense, looked upon by God as His family. They were His children, and, in that sense, He spoke of Himself as their Father.

Here, in this Letter of transition from the old Israel to the new, that idea is carried over into the spiritual realm:

"For it became him, for whom are all things, and through whom are all things, in bringing many sons unto glory, to make the author of their salvation perfect through sufferings. For both he that sanctifieth and they that are sanctified are all of one: for which cause he is not ashamed to call them brethren, saying,

"I will declare thy name unto my brethren,

"In the midst of the congregation will I sing thy praise. And again, I will put my trust in him. And again, Behold, I

and the children which God hath given me." (Hebrews ii.
10-13).

You will notice a whole list of quotations from the Old
Testament in that connection. Formerly it related to the
old Israel. That Israel has now been set aside and God is
taking up in a new way this principle of family life in
relation to Himself. His Son is *"the firstborn among many
brethren"* (Romans viii. 29) and we are *"sons of God,
through faith, in Jesus Christ"* (Galatians iii. 26).

You have probably noticed that the very first idea of
God was a family—the idea was born in His heart. This
is not some official society or institution. The deepest
thing in God's heart about us is to have us as His children,
and you, who know the Bible, will be able to quote to
yourself many passages, such as: *"Like as a father pitieth
his children, so the Lord pitieth them that fear him"* (Psalm ciii.
13). We could build up a tremendous mountain of
references to God as Father and to His people as His
children. He could have made an organization of people
into a kind of society. He could have called some from
one place and some from another, given them the title
of some denomination and said: 'Now you are members
of this denomination. You are formed into this organization.' But God never had any such idea. His idea is a
family, and the Lord Jesus said that He came into this
world especially to reveal God as Father—*"I kept them
in thy name which thou hast given me . . . I made known unto
them thy name"* (John xvii. 12, 26). The name of God
which was most on the lips of the Lord Jesus was 'Father',
and God has sent the Spirit of His Son into our hearts
whereby we say the same thing—*"Because ye are sons,
God sent forth the Spirit of his Son into our hearts, crying,
Abba, Father"* (Galatians iv. 6).

That is very elementary, but there is a very great battle

for this family conception. We do not worry very much if some organization gets broken up, not even if it is the 'United Nations', but we are always filled with grief and shame when a family breaks up. We feel that there is something about a family which carries a very sacred idea. What a bad thing it is when a family becomes divided! When children are against one another or against their parents, and the husband is against the wife and the wife against the husband. That is a special mark of the devil's work at the end of the dispensation! There is nothing more terrible in our time than the break-up of family life. The lists of divorces are most distressing, and poor children are left really without father or mother because of the break-up of the family. This is a blow at the deepest thing in the heart of God, but it does not stay there.

The most distressing aspect of this whole thing is in the family of God. There is nothing more terrible in this universe than the break-up of God's family. The devil does not mind our denominations and organizations, but he does object to this family matter! It is God's most cherished idea.

I think that is one of the most precious things about a time together like this. Here we are, representing quite a number of different nationalities. Many of us have never met before on this earth and have not yet had time to shake hands with one another, but we are all rejoicing here together as a family. The family spirit is the most precious thing, and it is the very hallmark of the heavenly Israel.

I have often said, in speaking about the heavenly Jerusalem as it is presented symbolically at the end of the Bible, that it has only one street. Our hymn-writers have led us astray over this, for they talk about the *streets* of

gold. The Bible says there is only one street of gold. So
we have to live in one street for all eternity! What do
you say about that? How are you going to get on with
your neighbours? Don't worry, it will be a very happy
thing to live on one street, for, you see, it will just be a
holy family. When the whole family is one it is not a bad
thing to live next door to one another!

Well, that is just a symbolic way of speaking about
this, but you know what it means. This is a spiritual
relationship: Father, big Elder Brother, the all-uniting
Holy Spirit . . . "holy brethren, companions in a heavenly
calling". It is a glorious thing to have companionship!

Thus this very first idea of God in the old Israel is
carried over spiritually to the new Israel.

(ii) *The house of God*

"*Moses indeed was faithful in all God's house as a servant,
for a testimony of those things which were afterward to be
spoken; but Christ as a son, over God's house; whose house
are we, if we hold fast our boldness and the glorying of our
hope firm unto the end*" (Hebrews iii. 5, 6).

Did you notice what that said? "*Moses indeed was
faithful in all God's house as a servant, for a testimony of those
things which were afterward to be spoken.*" When is the
afterward? It is *now*. "*Whose house are we.*" The house of
God is something which is carried over in principle by
God from the old to the new. Peter says that we are a
spiritual house—but there is one thing which needs to be
made quite clear here. When we use this word 'house',
we usually think of a place in which people live, but that
is not the meaning of the word here. I do not know
whether you can understand the change that I am going
to make, but do you know the difference between a
'house' and a 'household'? A household is quite a different

thing from a house. A household is two things: the people who dwell there and the order that exists. It is a house with a certain kind of order.

This is God's house, composed of His people who are under His order. He is a God of order. He is not only concerned to have things done, but to have them done in His way. It matters just as much to Him *how* things are done as to whether they are done at all. God's house is a house which is ordered by God. Everyone in it has to be in subjection to the Spirit of God and has to come under the headship of Jesus Christ.

We could spend very much time on the house of God! However, if you look into God's ordering of the life of Israel in the old dispensation, you will see how particular He was as to what was done and how it was done. God's spiritual and heavenly house was brought in on the Day of Pentecost, and He had His own new order. You will see how in those first days of the life of the Church two things were happening. God was demanding that His new order should be observed. Even the apostles had not come fully to recognize that new order. They were holding on to something of the old order, and when the Lord was moving toward the Gentiles in the case of Cornelius, the Gentile, Peter said: 'Not so, Lord. This is not according to the old order. I was not brought up in this way. The old system says I must not do that. Not so, Lord.' But the Lord is Lord of His own house, and He made it perfectly clear to Peter that He had brought in a new order. This was a new Israel. The Cross had made a great change: "*What God hath cleansed, make not thou common*" (Acts x. 15). The Cross has dealt with all uncleanness and we are moving on to a new basis.

Peter came to see that. Of course, this incident was not the end of the difficulty even for him, but I think that

E

when we come to his Letters we get to a Peter who has fully accepted the new order. "*A spiritual house*", says he, "*to offer up spiritual sacrifices*" (I Peter ii. 5).

But we were noting that in the Book of the Acts we have two things: there is the movement of the Spirit of God concerning the new order, but there is also the movement of the *evil* spirit against this new order. There is that terrible episode of Ananias and Sapphira who violated the new order of God's house. They brought in their own personal interests, and Peter summed it up in this way: "*Why hath Satan filled thy heart to lie to the Holy Ghost?*" (Acts v. 3). On that terrible day the new order was upset. Satan struck a blow at this new Israel, but to show how jealous God was for His heavenly order, see what happened to those two! God has therefore laid down the principle very clearly, and He is very jealous for His heavenly order.

Nothing but trouble can follow if we get out of God's order. While that is suspended everything is in confusion.

That is enough about the house of God for the time being—"*Whose house are we*".

(iii) *The heirs of God*

This matter is introduced with the Lord Jesus Himself: "*Whom He appointed heir of all things*" (Hebrews i. 1).

In verse fourteen of the first chapter we are spoken of as the heirs of salvation (" ... *for the sake of them that shall inherit salvation*").

In chapter six, verse seventeen, we are spoken of as "*the heirs of the promise*", and in the eighth chapter of the Letter to the Romans, verse seventeen, Paul says that we are "*heirs of God, and joint-heirs with Christ*".

In the earthly sense, Israel were to be God's heirs. The promise was made to Abraham that his seed would inherit the earth: God covenanted with him that his seed should be the possessors. Israel were to be God's heirs and they ought to have become joint-heirs with Jesus Christ. But they killed God's heir. They said, as in the parable spoken by the Lord Jesus, *"This is the heir: come, let us kill him"* (Matthew xxi. 38). They killed Him whom God had *"appointed heir of all things"*, and in so doing they robbed themselves of the inheritance.

Then the Church comes in—*"heirs of God and joint-heirs with Christ"*. The Church is now the heir to the promise made to Abraham, and this whole Letter to the Hebrews has to do with the inheritance, the great inheritance to which we are called as companions of the heavenly calling. The appeal to us in this Letter is: 'See that you do not miss the inheritance! The old Israel lost it through unbelief. You can lose the inheritance.' So the Letter uses Israel by way of illustrating the terrible possibility of Christians losing the inheritance.

Do you notice the little word 'if' which occurs so often? "We are become companions of Christ *if* we hold fast the beginning of our confidence firm unto the end" (Hebrews iii. 14): "Whose house are we, *if* we hold fast our boldness" (Hebrews iii. 6). That little word is a very big word! A lot hangs on it. We are not talking about the loss of eternal life, but of the *purpose* of salvation, which is a very much larger thing than just being saved. Paul says that there will be a lot of people who get into heaven having lost everything. All their life work will go up in smoke: *"He himself shall be saved; yet so as through fire"* (I Corinthians iii. 15). Everything but their salvation will be lost. Do you want to get into heaven "yet so as through fire"? No, this Letter says there is something more than being saved. There is a great inheritance, but we can miss it. Read the Letter again in the light of that.

However, our point here is that this principle of being heirs of God is carried over into the heavenly Israel.

(iv) *The city of God*

If you look into this Letter, you will find that the city is referred to on several occasions, such as: "*Ye are come . . . unto the city of the living God, the heavenly Jerusalem*" (Hebrews xii. 22).

The life of Israel was, of course, centred in the earthly Jerusalem. It was the centre of their unity. They were all united because of that city. That is why their males had to go up to Jerusalem so many times every year, and as they came, from the north, the south, the east and the west, a wonderful caravan, they sang the songs of Zion. Those Psalms about Zion are wonderful Psalms, and these men were glorying in their city, finding the expression of their national life there. It was the centre of their government. Their whole national life came out from the government in Jerusalem. Yes, Jerusalem was every-thing to them.

The writer of this Letter to the Hebrews is speaking about the approaching day, when that will have gone for ever, or for a whole dispensation. Jerusalem today is the very symbol of division. The Jews have one bit and the Arabs have another, and they cannot live in peace together. It is the symbol of disunion, and with God it does not stand. It has been passed over and God has brought in His heavenly Jerusalem—"*Ye are come . . . unto the city of the living God, the heavenly Jerusalem*".

We have been made "*to sit with him in the heavenly places, in Christ Jesus*" (Ephesians ii. 6). All our unity, as the new Israel, is centred in Him above. There will only be a true expression of unity amongst the Lord's people when they have a heavenly position. Our unity is in heaven, not on earth. Our government is from heaven, not from earth. Paul says we are *"fellow-citizens with the saints"* (Ephesians ii. 19), and that our *"life is hid with Christ in God"* (Colossians iii. 3).

Yes, the city exists. God's thought concerning it has been carried over to the spiritual Israel.

(v) *The flock of God*

These are all wonderful conceptions of the old Israel! If that Israel was God's family, the house of God, the heir of God, the city of God, so it was thought of as God's flock, God's sheep: *"Thou leddest thy people like a flock"* (Psalm lxxvii. 20). That idea, of course, lay behind the cry of the prophet Isaiah: *"All we like sheep have gone astray"* (Isaiah liii. 6). Israel was God's flock and He was their shepherd. We will dwell more fully upon that later (see part II)—it is indeed a very large matter in this new relationship to the Lord.

God has carried this over and it is a very precious thought of His concerning the heavenly Israel. We are *"the people of his pasture, and the sheep of his hand"* (Psalm xcv. 7), and when we come to the end of this Letter to the Hebrews we have this beautiful word: *"Now the God of peace, who brought again from the dead the great shepherd of the sheep . . . even our Lord Jesus"* (Hebrews xiii. 20).

There is a sense in which that spreads itself back over the whole Letter. The companions of Christ are His sheep: *"I am the good shepherd; and I know mine own, and mine own know me. . . . My sheep hear my voice, and I know them and they follow me: and I give unto them eternal life"* (John x. 14, 27, 28). That is a grand idea for sheep!

(vi) *The Kingdom of God*

We all know that Israel of old was God's kingdom,

over which He was king. Do you remember that when
they chose Saul to be the king, Samuel was very distressed
and went to the Lord about it? The Lord said to him:
"*They have not rejected thee, but they have rejected me, that
I should not be king over them*" (I Samuel vii. 7). The Old
Testament has a great deal to say about Israel being God's
kingdom.

Then we come into this new Israel: "*Wherefore,
receiving a kingdom that cannot be shaken*" (Hebrews xii. 28).
In the Greek the tense is: "Being in process of receiving
a kingdom which cannot be shaken". We are God's
kingdom, and people under His kingship and government.

We will have much more to say about this matter
later, but I think I have said enough now to show that
this is a very real thing. We have come in a spiritual way
into all that which was foreshadowed in the Israel of old.
The Lord Jesus said to that Israel: "*The kingdom of God
shall be taken away from you, and shall be given to a nation
bringing forth the fruits thereof*" (Matthew xxi. 43). Peter
said that we are "*a holy nation*" (I Peter ii. 9). We are the
inheritors of all that God ever meant for His people. In
us, that is, in His true Church of this dispensation, God
is in process of realizing all that which He had foreshadowed through many centuries.

We are a very privileged people. The great need of our
time is for Christians to know what God has called them
unto. Many do not know. You can go over this world and
find Christians in the majority who have no idea of
these things. They know that the Lord Jesus came into
the world as the Son of God and lived His wonderful life,
did His works, gave His teaching, died an atoning death
and rose again, has gone to heaven and is coming again;
but they do not know one bit of what it all means, that

is, what it is all unto, the great eternal purpose of God in it all. They are mostly quite ignorant of the things about which we have just been speaking, and that is why Christianity is in such a poor state today. They have not been given true instruction and have not a true understanding of God's great purpose in His Church through Christ Jesus. It is a very wonderful thing that we have come into in this dispensation.

CHAPTER SEVEN

THE TWO BEGINNINGS

IT WOULD BE a very wonderful thing if we could spend some time in seeing God's line right from the beginning up to Christ. There were many generations which came to an end, and in one place there is a large summary of what came and what finished. It says 'So-and-so lived, for so long, and he died.' That is said about a long list of people—they lived and then they died. However, right through there is one line that is the living line, continuing straight through history up to Christ. You can follow that line quite clearly, although, at times, it seemed to go under ground.

At a certain point in that movement of God, we find ourselves in the presence of His beginning with Israel. It has moved from individuals to the point where the nation comes into view. Up to then the movement had been with individuals—Abel, Enoch, Noah. Then, when it reached Abraham the nation came on the horizon, that is, the Israel of history, of this earth.

We are going to note how God began with Israel, and how the principle of that beginning is transferred to the new, heavenly Israel in Christ. It is very impressive to find that the beginning of the first Israel is in the New Testament, in the Book of the Acts. Note that, for it is a significant thing. The Book of the Acts is the link between the old and the new: the focal point of the transition from the one to the other is there. Interestingly enough, it is in the discourse of the martyr, Stephen. The new Israel received a great impetus by his death.

The first thing that Stephen said to the old Israel was: "*The God of glory appeared unto our father Abraham, when he was in Mesopotamia*" (Acts vii. 2). . . . "*The God of glory appeared.*" That was the first movement toward the old Israel, and that is exactly the first movement toward the new Israel: and we find that beginning in the New Testament.

We turn again to the Gospel by John: "*In the beginning was the Word . . . and the Word became flesh and tabernacled among us*": now note! "*and we beheld his glory*" (John i. 1, 14—R.V. margin). Then turn again to the Letter to the Hebrews: "*God . . . hath at the end of these days spoken unto us in his Son . . . the effulgence of his glory*" (Hebrews i. 1-3) . . . "*The God of glory appeared . . . and hath at the end of these days spoken unto us in his Son . . . the effulgence of his glory.*"

First of all, then, God is breaking into human history. That is how it was with the first Israel. Away there, in Ur of the Chaldees, a pagan country with two thousand other gods, the God of glory broke in and changed the course of history. Thus He took His first step toward the securing of Israel.

The first chapter of John shows the God of glory breaking into human history in a new way.

That, of course, is in the Bible, both in the Old and New Testaments, and you may have taken it in mentally, viewing it in an objective way. But you must just take hold of that and let it apply to you personally, because it relates to you and to me. You and I are called by God to be the companions of Christ in a heavenly calling and this belongs to all of us. The very beginning of our history as God's heavenly Israel is His intervention in our lives. Perhaps it was just as unexpected to some of us as it was to Abraham in Ur of the Chaldees. We were living our lives in this world, were mixed up in the course of things here and were ruled by the god of this world. We were just there, one in a great crowd . . . and then God broke in. When God breaks into a life there is no doubt about it. It is a turning-point in our history, and the nature of the change is that we no longer belong to this world. We have become members of a new Israel, of a heavenly people with a new spiritual nature. It may not have been with us just as it was with Abraham, but it is essential for every one of us to know that God has entered into our human history. In the first place it was not something from our side, but it was from God's side. He took the initiative, perhaps in a wonderful way, or in a very simple way. It may belong to a moment in time, or it may belong to days, weeks or months. However, the fact is that God came in where we were. How did God come in? How should we put it, if we wanted to put it into words? Well, it says here about the old Israel: "*The God of glory appeared*". Could you put it like that in your experience?

These words in the New Testament explain that. God came in Jesus Christ, and in Him is the glory of God. And as we have seen Jesus Christ, so we have come into touch with the God of glory. In the words of the Letter to the Hebrews: "*God . . . hath . . . spoken unto us in his Son*". All those who know that Jesus Christ has come into their lives really do know that the God of glory has come in. And so John, after saying that "*the Word became flesh and tabernacled among us*", says, "*and we beheld his glory, glory as of the only begotten from the Father*".

And what is the glory? John goes on to say "*full of grace and truth*". You will notice that in the New Testament grace and glory always go together. If you want to know what is the glory of God, well, it is the grace of God, and if you want to know what is the grace of God, it is the glory of God. It is the glory of God to be gracious. He glories in being gracious, and when you know the grace of God, then you know the glory of God. The glory of God will always come to us along the line of grace, and so, because of grace, we shall be able to say: *"We beheld his glory"*.

Perhaps you know that that word 'glory' is one of the big words in John's Gospel. If you have never done so, I advise you to go through the Gospel and underline that word.

(Now, just a little word to the young Christians who have not yet done a lot of Bible study. I had not thought of saying this, but perhaps it will be helpful. I do not profess to know a great deal about the Bible, indeed, I know very little of it, but I will tell you how I started to study it. I bought a box of coloured pencils and a new Bible. I started first with John's Gospel and I gave a certain colour to the same word through the Gospel. Of course, I always put green where the word 'life' is found! You see it all around—green speaks of life. Wherever the word 'glory' appears I put blue—that is the colour for heaven. I put red whenever anything to do with the blood or the Cross appeared—and so I went on. I had a wonderful result in the Gospel of John when I had finished! That is only a suggestion, but I hope that you may find it a helpful one. There are a lot more colours than those three!)

We are saying that 'glory' is one of John's great words, and all the references in his Gospel to Christ's glory are related to His super-natural person and His super-natural power. When John wrote *"We beheld his glory"* it was

many years after the Lord Jesus had come and gone.
John's Gospel is one of the last books of the New
Testament. All the other Apostles had probably gone to
the Lord when John wrote it. So he was looking back
over all that history and putting his impressions into
words, and as he thought of the Lord Jesus, His life, His
work, His teaching and everything else about Him, he
summed it all up in this: "*We beheld his glory*".

How did John behold the glory of the Lord Jesus? he
did so on many occasions and by a whole series of
humanly impossible situations.

(That is another line of study for you! Go to the Gospel
by John and see how many impossible situations you can
find.)

The Gospel is just full of impossible situations. There is
the marriage in Cana, when the wine failed. Humanly,
that is an impossible situation. Then there is Nicodemus—
and what is it that he is saying? "*How can a man be born
when he is old?*" (John iii. 4). An impossible situation!
Think of the woman of Samaria. She had tried everything to find satisfaction. An impossible situation! And
you can go right on like that. In all these situations Jesus
came in and turned the impossible into actuality. Thus
it says at the end of the account of the marriage in Cana:
"*This beginning of his signs did Jesus in Cana of Galilee, and
manifested his glory*" (John ii. 11). That was the principle
which governed everything. It does not always say so in
those words, but if you went back with that woman of
Samaria into the city and heard her shouting to all the
people: "*Come, see a man, which told me all things that ever
I did: can this be the Christ?*" (John iv. 29), you would
conclude that she had beheld His glory.

So you go right on to Lazarus. Jesus said: "*This sickness is not unto death, but for the glory of God, that the Son*

of God may be glorified thereby" (Jhn xi. 4). And in the difficulty being faced by the sisters when they could not altogether accept the fact that their problem was going to be solved at once, and they said: *"I know that he shall rise again in the resurrection at the last day"* (John xi. 24), Jesus replied: *"Said I not unto thee, that if thou believedst, thou shouldest see the glory of God?"* (John xi. 40). You see, the glory of God in Jesus Christ related to what God could do that no one else could do. It was the supernatural person and power of the Son of God.

That is the glory of God: and that is why we sometimes have such a difficulty in getting through. Perhaps you have often been troubled because of the difficulty some soul has in getting through to the Lord? It almost seems as though the Lord does not want to save them. They go through difficulties, sometimes for days, weeks or months, and all the time they are arguing and bringing up their problems, but nothing seems to happen. Then, at last, it does happen and they come through. Why is that? God is emphatically saying: 'This is going to be of Me, and not of yourself.' No man or woman can save himself or herself, even with all the goodwill of other people to help. The salvation of a soul is an impossible thing but for God, and He sees to it that it is put upon the supernatural basis. He very often does not come in until we have come to the point of despair—but He does come in then.

And what is true about salvation is so often true about our spiritual history. Again and again we are brought to the point where situations are quite impossible where man is concerned. We find we cannot solve that problem ourselves, or change that situation. If we were people of this world we might be able to do it, but somehow or other, because we are the Lord's people, it just does not

work. All our cleverne fails. Naturally there is no reason
why we should not g on, but the fact is that we just do
not. We try everything and are greatly perplexed. We
are being brought more and more to despair, and finally
to the point where we say: 'Well, only the Lord can do
this!'—and that i exactly what the Lord has been
working for. When the God of glory appears, He appears
as the God of glory. Do you see the point? Well, I said
that the word 'glory' in John's Gospel is connected with
the super-natural power of Jesus Christ, and we can only
learn who Jesus is by coming up against situations in
which He is the only one who can help us. The more
we go on to learn about the Lord Jesus the more
impossible will life be, and situations become, on this
earth.

That is the beginning of the God of glory.

Note the next thing: God's glory in Abraham reached
its climax in sonship. There were many things in the life
of Abraham when the God of glory needed to come in,
and so we read that in different situations 'the Lord
appeared unto Abraham'. However, the peak of all
God's appearances to Abraham was in connection with
Isaac—that is, it was bound up with this matter of sonship. The covenant of God with Abraham was going to
be realized along the line of sonship, and all God's
purposes in him were bound up with Isaac. Of course, at
the beginning Isaac was an impossibility, but at the end
he was a still greater impossibility—"*Take now thy son,
thine only son, whom thou lovest, even Isaac, . . . and offer him
there for a burnt offering*" (Genesis xxii. 2). All the promise
and covenant are wrapped up in Isaac, who is to be slain
with a knife. This is an impossible situation! Isaac to die?
There is no possibility of another Isaac, indeed, I doubt
whether Abraham would have wanted another. It was

a matter of life or death to him and is a quite impossible situation if Isaac lies dead on the altar. But you know what happened! And you know what the New Testament says about that: *"Accounting that God is able to raise up, even from the dead; from whence he did also in a parable receive him back"* (Hebrews xi. 19).

Has anyone but God ever raised someone from the dead? Man can do a great deal in prolonging life, and he thinks he will reach the time when he will raise the dead. Well, we have not reached that time yet, and we shall see whether God will surrender His own one prerogative—that is, to bring back a departed spirit into a dead body. That is God's act and is resurrection and not resuscitation.

I was saying that the glory of God reached its climax in Abraham's case along the line of sonship. Later on we shall have to look at this more closely in connection with Lazarus, but let us come back to *our* beginning.

We turn to John again—*"We beheld his glory"*. How do we behold His glory? *"He came unto his own, and his own received him not. But as many as received him, to them gave he power to become sons of God"* (John i. 12—A.V.)—He gave them the authority to be sons. That is our history. We are able to say: 'By God's intervention I am a child of God.' Then you notice how John analyses this: *"which were born, not of blood, nor of the will of the flesh, nor of the will of man, but of God"* (John i. 13). We are children of God by His intervention and by a direct act on His part. We are born from above and are made children of God. The glory of God is revealed in Jesus Christ in sonship.

Are you glorying in the fact that you are a born again child of God?

This same John, many years later, wrote these words,

with a very full heart: "*Beloved, now are we children of God, and it is not yet made manifest what we shall be. We know that, if he shall be manifested, we shall be like him; for we shall see him even as he is*" (1 John iii. 2). And connected with that, John said: "*Behold, what manner of love the Father hath bestowed upon us, that we should be called children of God*" (1 John iii. 1).

It is a wonderful thing to be a child of God! John said so, and he knew what he was talking about.

The glory, then, is in sonship. And it is at that point that Israel comes into view: Abraham's seed through Isaac. It is the nation that is coming into view and, as we have said, God said to Pharaoh: 'Let my son go.' That word 'son' was a comprehensive word, meaning the whole nation. God saw that nation as one son and would not surrender one fragment, because sonship is such a complete thing. Pharaoh said 'Well, let the men go. Leave the women and children and the flocks and herds', but Moses said: 'Not one single hoof of one single animal shall be left behind.' God had said 'My son', and that included the nation.

CHAPTER EIGHT

THE ABIDING VOCATION

Before going further with our main point there are two
things that I want to say in parenthesis.

First, I want to correct a possible misunderstanding.
The heavenly and spiritual Israel, which is the Church of
Jesus Christ, is not an afterthought of God. It was not
brought in because Israel failed. Please be very clear
about that. There are those who teach that that is so.
They say that the Lord offered it to Israel, who refused it.
He had to do something and so He got the idea of a
Church. It was quite an afterthought, a kind of emergency
movement of God. That is entirely false to the whole of
the Bible, and it is one thing we are seeking to show in
these days. We have said that everything in the Old
Testament, including Israel, had Christ and the Church
in view. It was all leading on to Christ and the Church,
and they take up all the divine thoughts of the past and
embody them in themselves. The Church is the *eternal*
thing. It was in the heart of God before time was and was
chosen in Christ before the foundation of the world. The
Church is no afterthought of God: it is a *before*-thought.
God's Son is no emergency matter. He may have come
in at a time of emergency, but He was in view for this
particular work from all eternity. The Church was
eternally intended to be the Body of Christ.

Now I want you to keep that in mind in all that we are
saying. We believe that if Adam had not been disobedient

in unbelief he would have been 'conformed to God's
Son'; but his sin meant that he forfeited the divine
intention. In the same way Israel would have become
incorporated into the corporate expression of Christ, but
in unbelief and disobedience Israel forfeited that 'inheritance'. The Church universal stood eternally over
Israel. This is a very important matter.

The other thing that I want to emphasize is this: that
this new Israel, the Church, is essentially a spiritual thing,
as truly as Christ, here, now, is a spiritual matter. And
Christ *is* here in this world by the Spirit. As truly as
Christ is here—though no longer in physical presence
and on a temporal basis (we can only know Him and
have fellowship with Him spiritually)—so it is as to the
Church.

There has to be a revolution in the minds of many
Christians about this matter. That word 'Church' is
taken up and put on to almost anything. Forgive me!
I mean no offence, but we are dealing with very vital
matters. We hear of, speak of, this church and that
church—the Lutheran church, the Methodist church, the
Baptist church, the Anglican church—and how many
more? We speak of all these as *the* church. From heaven's
standpoint that is a lot of nonsense. From heaven's standpoint those are not the Church. They may represent one
or other aspect of truth, but not one of them has the whole
of the truth, and when you put them all together they
have not all of the truth. All the truth is in Jesus alone.

The Church is a spiritual thing. You cannot look upon
anything material, or on people in the flesh, and say:
'That is the church.' You are only in the Church in so far
as there is something of Christ in you. It is Christ *in* us
that makes the Church. You see, the Church is a unity in
Christ.

The Lord Jesus never looks upon so many loaves of bread all over the world when there is a gathering to His Table. I suppose that on the Lord's Day there may be thousands of loaves of bread being broken, and I do not know how many cups—but heaven never sees more than one loaf or more than one cup. The loaf is Christ, the cup is Christ, and by partaking we are united in Christ.

It is not quite certain whether the translators were correct—though there may be something in it—when they translated the words of the Lord Jesus at the supper. In the old version it says: "*This is my body, which is broken for you*" (I Corinthians xi. 24—A.V.) There may be very real truth in using that word 'broken'. Indeed, the Lord's body was broken, but the later translators have left that word out and have put: "*This is my body, which is for you*" (I Corinthians xi. 24—R.V.). Perhaps that later translation dismisses a false idea, for that word 'broken' has so often been taken to mean—'Here is one piece, there is another, and there is another'; pieces all over the world. Christ is *not* divided. Paul said: "*Is Christ divided?*" (I Corinthians i. 13). No, Christ is not divided. There may be a thousand pieces of the earthly loaf, but the heavenly loaf is one, and that is how heaven sees the Church.

The Church is a broken thing on the earth. It is broken into many pieces down here, but in heaven it is seen as one, and the sooner you and I see from heaven's standpoint the better. If this man or this woman is "in Christ", it does not matter whether he or she is in our denomination or not, whether he or she is in our sect or not. If they are "in Christ" they are part with all others in Christ.

Understand that the Church is a spiritual thing, not an earthly, temporal thing, and that is a very important thing for us to recognize; it is comprised of all who are born of the Spirit.

We have taken a lot of time before we come on to our particular point. We are doing this: Along one side we are tracing God's ways with the old Israel, and along the other side we are seeing that He takes the spiritual laws of that old Israel and perpetuates them in the new Israel. What He did in a temporal way with the first Israel, He is now doing in a spiritual way with the new Israel.

Our last word was that God's glory in Abraham reached its climax in sonship. Sonship in death and resurrection as represented by Isaac. Sonship is the climax of God's glory.

We are back in the Letter to the Hebrews now. What is the climax of that Letter and of all God's movement as contained in it? It is found in one fragment: *"Bringing many sons unto glory"* (Hebrews ii. 10). That is the climax of the glory of God. As it was in a temporal way with Abraham, so it is in a spiritual way with the new Israel.

But the idea of sonship did not begin with Abraham and Isaac. It only came out in them. It went right back before them—it was God's cherished secret from before times eternal. That secret has been lost in Abraham's seed after the flesh, but is taken up in Abraham's Seed after the Spirit.

You probably know that the Letters to the Romans and the Galatians are concerned with this very thing. The Apostle is saying just this in the Letter to the Romans, chapters nine, ten and eleven (all one section really). *"They are not all Israel, which are of Israel"* (Romans ix. 6) —'All the natural children of Abraham are not Israel. Israel is only the spiritual children of Abraham.'

When you go into the Letter to the Galatians that is explained very carefully, and Paul reduces it to this one thing. He refers to the promise made to Abraham: "*In thy seed shall all the nations of the earth be blessed*" (Genesis xxii. 18).

This is the thing that got Paul into a lot of trouble. He said: "*(God) saith not, And to seeds, as of many; but as of one, And to thy seed, which is Christ*" (Galatians iii. 16). It is not the many natural children of Abraham, but the spiritual children—and that is Christ and the companions of Christ.

Isaiah cried: "*He shall see his seed . . . he shall see of the travail of his soul*" (Isaiah liii. 10, 11), and this heavenly Jerusalem is the spiritual seed of Abraham, which is Christ and the 'born from above' ones.

The Letter to the Galatians teaches that the rest have gone. Even all the other children of Abraham are now set aside, and God recognizes only His spiritual children. This is taken up in this phrase which has governed our whole time: "*Wherefore, holy brethren, companions of a heavenly calling . . . we are become companions of Christ, if we hold fast the beginning . . . firm unto the end*" (Hebrews iii. 1, 14).

This spiritual and heavenly Israel is called "companions of a heavenly calling", and we will dwell upon that heavenly calling for a few minutes.

What was God's intention in this world concerning the first Israel? It was that they should mediate light and life to the nations. That was their divine calling—that the nations should receive life through their light; that they should be the channel of divine light and life to the nations of this world. We could take quite a lot of the Old Testament to show this, but we are going to use only one illustration.

You notice that all the sons of Israel were focused in one son. (Of course, when we speak of Israel now, we

mean Jacob.) That son was Joseph. If it had not been for
him that whole nation would have perished, and not
only the sons and families of Jacob, but all Egypt. In a
sense that world would have perished. God's strange,
sovereign dealings with Joseph brought him, through
death and resurrection, to the throne. Then his brothers
came to Egypt and he made himself known to them.
They went down before him in utter shame, began to
apologize and try to excuse themselves. Poor, miserable,
wretched fellows they were! But what did Joseph say?
*"Be not grieved, nor angry with yourselves, that ye sold me
hither: for God did send me before you to preserve life"*
(Genesis xlv. 5). Life and light came not only to all the
families of Jacob, but to Egypt, the world, through
Joseph. He was the inclusive representative of all his
brethren. God made him like that, and he sets forth this
truth that God intended all Israel of old to be a minister
of life and light to the whole world. That was Israel's
calling and what they were intended for in the old
dispensation. They were just down here by God's
appointment, right at the centre of the nations, in a
position of ascendancy, in order to mediate light and life
to the nations. Abraham's seed was intended to do that,
but that seed failed God, and instead of fulfilling their
calling, they contradicted it.

We need not dwell upon their failure. It is a dark and
terrible story. And for the last nearly two thousand years
they have been where the Lord Jesus said they would be:
*"The sons of the kingdom shall be cast forth into the outer
darkness: there shall be the weeping and gnashing of teeth"*
(Matthew viii. 12). That is the story of the earthly Israel,
as a nation, through all these past centuries. Thank God
for all those who have escaped from the outer darkness,
who are not weeping and gnashing their teeth, but are

rejoicing in Christ Jesus! But that is where the nation went, and the last stroke of that was in A.D. 70.

That is the dark side. But God had not finished with an Israel. He still had in view a 'Prince with God', for that is the meaning of the name 'Israel'. This heavenly, spiritual Israel to which you and I belong is called into the vocation of Joseph. God has transferred that in a spiritual way to us. We are here in this heavenly calling, this spiritual vocation to minister light and life to the world. That is to be our heavenly calling now, and that is why the Lord Jesus said to His new Israel: "*Go ye therefore, and make disciples of all the nations*" (Matthew xxviii. 19) . . . 'Begin at Jerusalem . . . Samaria . . . all Judaea . . . and unto the uttermost parts of the earth . . . and wherever you are your heavenly calling is to bring light and life from above.'

At the beginning the Church almost settled down in the earthly Jerusalem. They were very slow to move away from there, so the Lord took a big hammer and brought it down on the Church in that city. Then they were all scattered abroad; and the Lord said: 'I have finished with this earthly city. The new Jerusalem is above, and the new, heavenly calling is to all the nations.'

That is the heavenly calling of the spiritual Israel now, but that has to come to fulness afterward. That fulness is represented at the end of the Bible—"*the holy city, new Jerusalem, coming down out of heaven from God*" (Revelation xxi. 2). No, this is not a material and political world-centre. This is the Church. These are the companions of Christ represented in the symbolism of a city, and the last word about that city is this: "*And the nations shall walk amidst the light thereof . . . and on this side of the river and on that was the tree of life . . . and the leaves of the tree were for the* health *of the nations*" (Revelation xxi. 24,

xxii. 2). Did you notice that I changed a word? Our translation says "for the *healing* of the nations", but that is not correct. The nations will not need healing in eternity, thank God! But they will need their spiritual health ministered to.

Most of us here do not need saving. Remember, by the way, that the word 'salvation' in the original is the word 'health'. It is being in a state of good health. That is the meaning of the word 'salvation'—being in spiritually good health.

The nations then will be those that have had the Gospel and have responded: "*The earth shall be filled with the knowledge of the glory of the Lord, as the waters cover the sea*" (Habakkuk ii. 14), but right at the centre of the nations will be the Church, and through the Church light and life will go out to maintain the health of the nations.

So, when everything has been said and done, and you ·have gone right through the long, long story, at last you come to the end in the last chapter of history in the Book of the Revelation: and the last picture is of a heavenly Israel ministering light and life to the nations.

Perhaps some of you Bible students and you people who are interested in doctrine are troubled now with a question, in view of what I have said. 'Does he mean that the Church is one thing and that there are a lot of people who are not of the Church? In other words, is the city one thing and are the nations another?'

I am not going to enter on any argument over that, but I am going to bring you back to this Letter to the Hebrews for your answer. It is one little word of two letters: '*IF*'! "We are become companions of Christ *if* . . . ": "Whose house are we *if* . . . ". In one sense the whole Letter circles round that little word. It is not now a matter of salvation and getting into heaven. It is now a matter of that instrument of eternal vocation for all the rest. This is the height of the heavenly calling. I leave you to answer the question by studying this Letter again. It does *seem* to say that everyone will not be the city. If everyone is the city, where is the country? No, the city is the centre, the seat of administration, of government and of light. The whole country derives its values through the city. It does seem that that is the truth that is here. It is possible to get into heaven but not be of the city.

If you have trouble with that and you disagree with me—I can only say to you: 'Go back to the Word.' I cannot understand this Letter on any other ground, unless we admit that the warnings relate to salvation and not to inheritance. Why is it shot through and through with this urgency to go on? I do not believe that if you do not go on you forfeit your eternal life or sacrifice your salvation, but I do believe that if you do not go on you will forfeit your inheritance, and that is the teaching of this Letter as I see it. Why, the whole of the New Testament, after the Gospels, has this one object: to get Christians to go on, and to go on to full growth.

God put something into the very constitution of Abraham which had two effects. It made him a very discontented man. He was possessed of a *holy* discontent. He saw the land and God gave him flocks and herds in abundance, but all the time he was going up and down the land saying: 'This is not it. There is something more than this. I can never be satisfied with this.' In a right sense Abraham was a most discontented man.

On the other side, he had a vision of what ought to be. The New Testament calls it a heavenly country. (See Hebrews xi. 16.) He was looking for a city "*whose builder and maker is God*", and no city on this earth answered to what was in the heart of Abraham. Do you think I am exaggerating? Do you think I am making that up? What did Jesus say to the old Israel? *"Your father Abraham rejoiced to see my day; and he saw it, and was glad"* (John xiii. 56). Abraham saw right down the ages. He had a vision and nothing *in this world* could satisfy that vision. His heart was ever hungry and so he was a man who never settled down on this earth.

"Let us go on", says this Letter to the Hebrews. 'Let us not settle down, and let us never be satisfied with anything less than God's fulness.' That is its message.

In the end it is represented as a race. We are running a race and the goal and prize lie ahead. Let us not stop in the race and turn aside! *"Let us run with patience the race that is set before us, looking unto Jesus . . ."* (Hebrews xii. 1, 2). *"Your father Abraham rejoiced to see my day;" "Looking unto Jesus"*. Let us never settle down with anything less than God's fulness. *"Wherefore, holy brethren, companions of a heavenly calling."*

Where the Holy Spirit really has His place in a heart, that heart will be a 'going on' heart. It will never settle down to anything less than God's fulness.

There are two different kinds of dissatisfaction. There are those poor, miserable people who are never satisfied with anything. They are always discontented, and in a wrong way. We are not appealing for such people! But this spiritual discontent, this that says: *"Not that I have obtained, or am already made perfect . . . but one thing I do, forgetting the things which are behind . . . I press on toward the goal unto the prize of the high calling of God in Christ Jesus"* (Philippians iii. 12-14), is the nature of a truly Holy Spirit-governed life. It will always be pressing on to something more of the Lord. Such are the true heavenly seed of Abraham, the companions of a heavenly calling.

CHAPTER NINE

THE SUPERIORITY OF THE NEW POSITION

WE ARE NOW going to concentrate upon one aspect of the great transition: the superiority of the heavenly Israel to the earthly.

The writer of this Letter, whoever he was, was giving himself wholly to the immense superiority of what had come in with this dispensation. It was as though he said to himself: 'The time has come for someone to let these people know how superior is that which has come in with this dispensation. This final movement of God in the history of this world is greater than anything before.' So that is what he set himself to show to the people of his day. But God meant it for more than that: He meant it for His people for all time.

No one knows who wrote this Letter. Many names have been mentioned. Some have been very certain about who it was, and then someone else has come along and upset that certainty. Some have been sure that Paul wrote it, while others have very nearly proved that he did not. Some have thought that Apollos wrote it, and others have said that it was Barnabas. Apollos, it was said, was a man *"mighty in the Scriptures"* (Acts viii. 24), and it certainly did require such a man to write this document! Barnabas was a Levite, and he knew all about the Levitical system of the Old Testament, so he would be a good one to write the book. As for Paul, well, of course, he was the perfect master both of Judaism and of Christianity, and it needed a man like that to write this book. If Stephen had not been martyred I would have chosen him, because I think that in his last great discourse you have all the substance of the Letter to the Hebrews.

Well, we cannot say. Perhaps the Lord has never thought it to be very important to settle a human name upon it, but rather to make everything of "God . . . hath spoken."

We are touching very old and well-worn ground when we remind you of the place that the word 'better' has in this Letter. It occurs more often here than in all the rest of the New Testament put together.

(Here is a study for the beginners in Bible Study. Get out your box of coloured pencils, choose a colour that you think is suitable to 'better', and underline that word through this Letter.)

This word occurs thirteen times in the Letter and always in a very instructive connection. I will just mention the references:

Chapter i. 4—"Better than the angels". (That is a high place at which to begin!)

Chapter vi. 9—"We are persuaded better things of you".

Chapter vii. 19—"A better hope".

Chapter vii. 22—"A better covenant".

Chapter viii. 6—"A better covenant" and "better promises".

Chapter ix. 23—"Better sacrifices".

Chapter x. 34—"A better possession".

Chapter xi. 16—"A better country".

Chapter xi. 35—"A better resurrection".

Chapter xi. 40—"Some better thing".

Then, alongside of that, you can put:

Chapter xii. 24—"The blood of sprinkling that speaketh better than that of Abel".

In chapter i. 4 and viii. 6 there are the words "more excellent", and in chapter i. 4, chapter iii. 3 and chapter x. 25 there is the phrase "by so much . . . more".

So that word is a key to the Letter. Everything here is better than it has ever been before. And we can come back with that to our own key words: *"Holy brethren, companions of a heavenly calling"*—called to something so much better than has ever been in the history of this world.

Let us remind ourselves of why this Letter was written.

In the first place, it was written to save these Christians from spiritual declension or spiritual arrest. For various reasons they were being tempted to draw back. You will remember that those words occur in a warning: *"If any man draw back, my soul shall have no pleasure in him"* (Hebrews x. 38—A.V.). It is a terrible thing to get into a place where the Lord has no pleasure in you, to lose the pleasure of the Lord! And it was to prevent these Christians from getting into such a position that this Letter was written.

Some of these Christians were inclined just to stand still and not go on any further, so that their spiritual life would be arrested and they would no longer go on and grow. They would become "stand-still" Christians—'As it was, so it is now'. Nothing of the future was governing them. So this Letter was written to save them from going back or from standing still.

However, we have already pointed out that there was another reason: It was to carry these Christians through a time of great trouble which was coming. Evidently this Letter was written very shortly before the destruction of Jerusalem. Perhaps the writer already saw the signs of that, but, whether he did or not, the Holy Spirit saw what was coming. He knew that a time of great testing was coming to these Christians, when all that in which they had trusted on this earth was going to be shaken, so He led this writer to write this Letter. It was intended to be a strength to them and salvation in a time of trouble. And the method of so ministering help to them was to show again the greatness of the Lord Jesus, the greatness of the heavenly calling, and how great a thing it is to be companions of Christ and of the heavenly calling. So the writer sets out to bring into view the Lord Jesus in His superiority to all who had gone before. But in doing so, he does another thing, and this is a very interesting matter. He says: 'Down through the past ages there have been men who have had great difficulties, many discouragements and trials,' and he mentions Abraham.

Now Abraham had indeed a difficult life. There was the difficulty of the postponed promise—God's promises did not seem to be in the way of fulfilment. He was taking such a long time to fulfil His word. We all know something about that difficulty! We are in a hurry and God is not—He seems to have all time at His disposal. Our trouble is: 'Oh, if only the Lord would hurry up!', and I suppose our prayers are so often marked by one word: 'Lord, hasten it!'

If any man knew about having to be patient, it was Abraham! There was this difficulty of God taking so much time to fulfil His promises, and Abraham sometimes broke down under that. On one occasion he left the land of promise and went to Egypt—and there he found himself in still greater trouble. He had to tell a lie to get out of it.

This matter was a very real test to Abraham. I think there are signs that his wife was not always in sympathy with him. When they were both old and the Lord said that they would have a son, Sarah, who was in her tent, heard and "*laughed within herself*" (Genesis xviii. 12). The

Lord was angry, and Abraham had to rebuke Sarah. Well, we must have full sympathy with Sarah. She was being hard put to it by the way the Lord was taking her husband and she was not always able to see as he saw, or feel as he felt. Perhaps, for that reason, Abraham had a certain measure of spiritual loneliness in his life.

Then what about that young man Lot? He was just a lot of trouble! He certainly did not share Abraham's vision! His vision was all on this earth, his ambitions all for the present, and you know well his story and what a thorn he was in the side of Abraham.

We could add other things to the painful story. Abraham's was not an easy life. But, do you know, the New Testament says that Abraham *rejoiced*! Why did he do so? Why did he rejoice in tribulation? Jesus Himself tells us the answer to that: "*Your father Abraham rejoiced to see my day; and he saw it and was glad*" (John viii. 56). In some way Abraham had seen the Lord Jesus, had seen the day of the Lord Jesus, and that had got him through all his troubles.

You know, there is more in this Letter to the Hebrews about what Abraham saw. He had seen in the spirit a heavenly country, and was looking for it. He had seen "*the city which hath the foundations, whose builder and maker is God*" (Hebrews xi. 10). Abraham had seen the day of Jesus Christ. You will remember that this writer said: "*Ye are come unto . . . the heavenly Jerusalem*" (Hebrews xii. 22). Abraham had seen that, and, having seen the Lord Jesus, he was able to go on and rejoice in a long life of trial.

What about Moses? Did he have any troubles? Well, we can make a long story about the troubles of Moses! He had to carry a very heavy burden, and there was a time when he nearly lost heart. He said to the Lord: "*I am not able to bear all this people alone, because it is too heavy for me*" (Numbers xi. 14). Moses often had to go back to the Lord like that and say: 'You have asked me to do something which is more than I can do.' He had very many trials through forty long, weary years. But we have this word here: "*He endured, as seeing him who is invisible*" (Hebrews xi. 27). Who was the "him" that Moses was seeing? Notice what this Letter to the Hebrews says! When Moses was in Pharaoh's palace and saw his own brethren being persecuted, he decided that he was going to take sides with them, and this Letter says: "*Choosing rather to be evil entreated with the people of God*" —and now comes a wonderful thing—"*accounting the reproach of Christ greater riches than the treasures of Egypt*" (Hebrews xi. 25, 26). The *reproach of Christ*! What did Moses know about Christ? Somehow he had seen Him and seen that these Hebrew people were called in relation to Him, so "*He endured, as seeing him who is invisible*".

This is a point at which our minds have to get adjusted. Perhaps we have the idea that when Jesus came into this world, that was the beginning of Him, but the Word of God makes it perfectly clear that Jesus Christ was present in the days of Abraham and Moses. Indeed, the Word says that He was present in the creation of the world: "*All things were made by him*" (John i. 3). He was there all the time. He was the One who appeared again and again and they did not recognize Him. He appeared to Abraham, to Moses, to Joshua, to Gideon . . . yes, this same Christ was there, active all the time. He did not just begin when He was born in Bethlehem. It was then that He came into this world in human form.

Do you think that is exaggerating? Well, let us come to our Letter to the Hebrews: "*Jesus Christ . . . the same yesterday, and to-day, yea and for ever*" (xiii. 8). I have left out one little word—"Jesus Christ *is* the same . . . ": He *is* yesterday, He *is* today and He *is* tomorrow. There is no yesterday, today or tomorrow with Jesus. Yesterday was the day of the old dispensation. When this writer wrote this Letter it was 'today' in which he lived, the new dispensation that had just begun. 'Today' is the period between Christ going back to heaven and His coming again. We have seen already how one phrase is quoted three times in this Letter, and it is brought over from yesterday to today: "*To-day if ye shall hear his voice, harden not your hearts*" (Hebrews iii. 7, 8). That is a message for this dispensation. 'Tomorrow' is for ever, and it is going to be the same Jesus Christ.

So the writer of this Letter is saying: 'Jesus Christ was back there in yesterday. He was in the past dispensation. And it is the same Jesus Christ that we know today. And He will be the same Jesus Christ for ever.'

Do you notice how many quotations from the Old Testament there are in the first chapter of this Letter? We cannot stay to look at them, but the Old Testament is used here a very great deal, and the quotations are concerning Christ, so that, in the first place, it is quite clear that He was in the Old Testament. He was being spoken about then and was present in the minds of Old Testament writers. There are quotations from David. Jesus Christ was very much in the mind of David. The words "*Thou art my Son, this day have I begotten thee*" were first written by him (Psalm ii. 7), and there is much more like that.

There are very many quotations from the Old Testament at the beginning of this Letter, which simply shows that Jesus Christ was present then. And that Jesus Christ is brought over from yesterday to today. This writer is just saying: 'That Jesus Christ of the prophets and the

G

men of old is this One of whom I am writing today.'
The first chapter of the Letter just takes up all that about
Christ and brings it here into the present—and it is the
same Jesus Christ.

We have hardly begun to see the superiority of this
today over yesterday. We have only sought to do one
thing, and that is what this writer set out to do: to show
that to get through trouble and testing you need to have
a large conception of the Lord Jesus. To get through to
the end in victory will depend upon what kind of Christ
our Christ is to us.

The writer realized that these Christians were finding
the 'race' rather long and difficult, and their need was
the most testing thing in spiritual life—patience. "*Ye
have need of patience*", says the writer, "*that, having done
the will of God, ye may receive the promise*" (Hebrews x. 36).
Later he says: "*Let us run with patience the race that is set
before us*" (Hebrews xii. 1). What is the real strength of
patience? Oh, it is so easy to say to people: 'Now, be
patient. Don't be in a hurry. Things will turn out all
right.' But this writer did not just say to these Christians:
'Now be patient!' He said: "Let us run with patience the
race . . . " It will test our patience, will call for a lot of
patience, but the thing that will keep our patience strong
is this—"*Looking off unto Jesus*" (Hebrews xii. 2). If we
look at ourselves we will give up the race, and we shall
do so if we look at other people. There are a lot of people
who will make us give up the race. If we look around us
on the world we shall lose patience. And so we like the
true translation of this phrase. Some versions just have
"*Looking unto Jesus*". Well, that is all right, but the real
version is: "Looking *off* unto Jesus". You must take your
eyes off yourself. You must positively refuse to look at
yourself. You must train yourself in the habit of refusing

to look at yourself. Every time you are tempted to do so you have to say: 'No! I shut my eyes to that.' You must not have your eyes on those Christians who are disappointing. You must remember that the very best Christians are only human, after all. It is a very dangerous thing to think of any man or woman as being infallible.

Perhaps Paul was very near to doing that once. You know, he owed a very great deal to Barnabas. It was Barnabas who went off to find Paul and brought him back. I think that when even some of the Apostles saw Saul of Tarsus come in through the door they drew back. They were all suspicious of this man and they drew back from him. But Barnabas took him by the hand and brought him in, saying: 'Don't be afraid, brothers. He has met our Lord Jesus. He is now a companion of Jesus Christ. He is one with us.' And so they received him.

It was Barnabas who brought Paul to Antioch, a church that was in great need at that time. They needed a very strong minister, and off went Barnabas, saying: 'I know the man.' He brought Saul to Antioch and introduced him to his life ministry.

Paul owed a lot to Barnabas, of whom it was said: *"He was a good man, and full of the Holy Spirit"* (Acts xi. 24). Perhaps Paul put Barnabas on a high pedestal! And then came that terrible day when Barnabas fell off that pedestal. You know of the division between the Jewish and Gentile Christians and that the new order of Christ demanded that they should be all one, eating and drinking together. Peter had learnt that lesson at the house of Cornelius, but then that day came when this whole question of Jews and Gentiles eating and drinking at the same table arose. It was a very strong dispute and a very critical day. James and some of the others from Jerusalem went down—and Peter withdrew from the

table. He was afraid of James and of those others from
Jerusalem! He said: 'I must not let these senior brothers
see me eating with Gentiles.' And Paul says: "*And the
rest of the Jews dissembled likewise with him; insomuch that
even Barnabas was carried away with their dissimulation*"
(Galatians ii. 13). 'Just think of it—*Barnabas*! I never
thought Barnabas would do a thing like that! I thought
he was far above anything of that sort.' I am sure it was
a very great blow to Paul's confidence in men, but if
he had continued to keep his eyes on Barnabas no one
knows what would have happened. He had to look off
from Barnabas to Jesus.

Paul was always having to do that. In many ways and
situations he had to take his eyes off and look unto Jesus.
There is a real touch of Paul in this Letter to the Hebrews
—"Looking off unto Jesus". Whoever actually wrote
this Letter, the shadow of Paul is over it. His influence
is everywhere. And certainly he was called upon to look
off unto Jesus.

Now that is a very vital lesson for us to learn. We have
to do that again and again in our Christian life. If we get
our eyes upon anything but the Lord Jesus we just go to
pieces. Have all respect for God's saints. I am not saying
that you have to eye every servant of God with suspicion
and be saying all the time: 'Well, of course, he is not
perfect, you know.' Give honour to whom honour is
due, but never build your faith upon any man, however
good he may be.

And as for ourselves—well, I think perhaps we are
more tempted to look at ourselves than anything else!
This is one of our real Christian exercises. We have
continually to remove our eyes from ourselves and
everything to do with ourselves. There is nothing more
discouraging than this self of ours, and nothing more

misleading. Our own judgments are all wrong, and so are our thoughts and ideas. They are not God's thoughts.

We must take our eyes off ourselves, but not look out into space and be vacant. *"Look off unto Jesus"*, and you know how that sentence is finished—*"Jesus, the author and finisher of our faith"*. Did you start this thing? Are you a Christian because *you* decided to be a Christian? Well, the Lord help you if that is so! No, He started this thing. Are you not glad that you can say: 'It was the Lord who found me. It was the Lord who put His hand on me.'? What He said is very true: *"Ye did not choose me, but I chose you"* (John xv. 16). He was the author of our faith, and it says that He is the finisher—He will finish it.

When we get to heaven we will be full of wonder that we ever did get there! We will just look at one another and say: 'Well, we are here! It is a wonderful story! How we got here we do not know. We have thought a thousand times that we never would get here. We had given up all hope—but we are here!' And it will be because Jesus is the finisher. Believe that, dear friend! In the day of your despair and difficulty, look off unto Jesus. He has said: *"Where I am, there shall also my servant be"* (John xii. 26). Though it takes a thousand miracles, He will work them to get us there. Do believe it! Take hold of it with both hands and trust Him to see you right through to glory, for that is one of the great things in this Letter: *"Bringing many sons unto glory"* (Hebrews ii. 10). That means you and it means me.

CHAPTER TEN

THE SUPERIORITY OF THE NEW
POSITION (*continued*)

IN OUR LAST message we only made a beginning with this matter—and when we say 'we made a beginning' as we come almost to the end of the Conference, it is quite evident that we are going to have twelve basketfuls over when we have finished! We really have not sounded the full depth of this Letter to the Hebrews, and there is so much more that could extend us for a long time. Perhaps that is how it ought to be. We do not want to come to an end. We want to feel that the land is a land of far distances, and that the Lord can lead us into it, even without a Conference.

Well, we are now going on a little way further into that land—the land of the superiority of this dispensation over all past dispensations.

We are now at the supreme matter in the Letter, and, therefore, the supreme matter in the dispensation: that is, how much higher and fuller is that which has come in with the Lord Jesus than ever came in in old time.

You will see, right at the beginning of the Letter, that this is the dispensation of God's Son, and the dispensation of Him in a new personal manifestation. We believe that He was present in the old dispensation and appeared to men in other forms, but this Letter says that He has come in a new form. So it begins with the manifested presence of God's Son. The first verse says that in the old dispensation men met God in "*divers portions and in divers manners*", and God met men and men met God in the prophets. Now the prophets were the servants of God, and men met God through His servants. In this dispensation they meet Him in His Son personally. There is a statement that "*God was in Christ*" (II Corinthians v. 19), so the 'Son' implies the 'Father', and the 'Son of God' implies God. So we meet God in the Son and not now in servants.

This reaches absolute fulness in the matter of divine revelation. "*For it was the good pleasure of the Father that in him (the Son) should all fulness dwell*" (Colossians i. 19). There is nothing more to be added.

Do not take these as just words. Do understand that in every fragment there is this truth: In the dispensation in which you and I are now living God has come to us in all His fulness. There is no more to be added. In His Son we have the absolute fulness of God, and it is out of that fulness that He speaks to us in His Son. God has only one Son in that sense—His *only*-begotten Son, which means that there is no one to come after Him. Therefore, God's last word is in His Son. The Son brings both the fulness and the finality of God. It is that which gives the solemnity to this whole Letter. It says: 'If you fail to hear the voice of the Son there will never be another voice for you. God is never going to speak by another voice. God hath spoken in His Son, and He is never going to speak by any other means.' Hence this Letter contains this word of warning and of exhortation: 'Because this is the fulness and this is the end, be sure that you give heed.'

But it is not only God speaking in His Son. That is a way of speaking, but God's speaking is always His acting. In this dispensation God is active in and through His Son. To come into touch with the Lord Jesus is more than coming into touch with a teaching: it is coming into touch with a living, active Person. 'It is God with whom we have to do.' It is a glorious thing to come into touch with God in Christ—but it says here that "*it is a fearful thing to fall into the hands of the living God*" (Hebrews x. 31). No, it is not a book, a teaching, a philosophy: it is a living, positive, powerful Person. It is no other than God in action.

If you have any doubt about that, just remember the Book of the Acts. It is called the Acts of the Apostles, but everyone knows that name is wrong, for only three or four Apostles are in view after the first chapter. The others are spoken of at the beginning and then you hear no more about them. It is not the book of the Acts of the Apostles, but the book of the Acts of God in Jesus Christ by the Holy Spirit—and it is indeed a book of *acts*! Whatever teaching there is comes out of the acts.

So, in Hebrews, the Son is introduced, presented, and then described. And it is a wonderful description! But we ask: 'Who is this Son?', for His name is not mentioned until we come to chapter two, verse nine. Until then it is the God without a name. Who is this Son? Well, it tells us for the first time in that verse: "*We behold him who hath been made a little lower than the angels, even Jesus*". Perhaps it seems a very simple thing to say that Jesus is this Son, and this Son is Jesus, but possibly you do not recognize a certain thing about this: it is very rarely, after His resurrection and ascension, that He is called Jesus. After He has gone back to heaven He is usually 'the Lord Jesus', 'Jesus Christ our Lord', or 'our Lord Jesus Christ'. He is given His full title when He is enthroned in heaven, so if someone comes right back from that and just uses the title 'Jesus', you know that His humiliation and the purpose of that humiliation are

being referred to. It has to do with His work on earth
for our redemption.

So look at this verse again: "We behold him who hath
been made a little lower than the angels, even Jesus,
because of the suffering of death". Jesus was the name of the
one who suffered death, tasted death for every man—
and it was the Son of God who did that. He it was who
as *Jesus* tasted death for every man, and that is the Son
who is introduced here. He is identified by His name—
Jesus . . . "*Thou shalt call his name* JESUS: *for it is he that
shall save his people from their sins*" (Matthew i. 21).

Then the next thing is the position and function of the
Son. In the second verse of the first chapter of this
Letter you have this: "(*God*) *hath at the end of these days
spoken unto us in his Son, whom he appointed heir of all
things, through whom also he made the worlds*". This Son,
known to us as Jesus, is by God's appointment the *heir of
all things*. All things are to come to Him by right of
God's appointment.

Please do not be weary with me. This is one of the first
things said about the dispensation in which you and I live.
It does not look very much like it now, for "*we see not
yet all things subjected to him*" (Hebrews ii. 8), but it says
here emphatically that He is the "heir of all things",
so everything *has* to come to Him in the end. God is
going "*to sum up all things in Christ, the things in the
heavens, and the things upon the earth*" (Ephesians i. 10).

If we were speaking in human language we would
put it like this: there was somewhere in the past eternity
an occasion when the Godhead had a conference, to
discuss the future of everything that was going to be
made. There the Father said: 'I make My Son the heir
of all things. I appoint Him My heir, and I decree that
all things shall in the end come into His possession.'

Now we are dealing with the all-mighty and eternal God, and when He decides a thing like that *nothing* can prevent it. "Whom he *appointed* heir of all things"—but He did not leave it there. He turned to the Son (of course, this is only our way of speaking) and said: 'Now I am going to use You as the agent in making all things'— "through whom also he made the worlds". This Son, whom we know as our Saviour and Lord, was God's agent in the creation of the worlds.

Then it says a third thing, and this is something so difficult to understand: This Son upholds "*all things by the word of his power*" (Hebrews i. 3). Things do not collapse because He is "upholding all things by the word of his power". And things will not collapse until He says they should do so.

If that is true then it is something very wonderful for us. We are hearing so much about the disintegration of the universe and the blowing to pieces of this world. A lot of people are getting very frightened about this. If what is here is true, the universe and the world can never go to pieces until Jesus says so! Men may get very near to doing it, and then it recedes. It just does not happen. It has been like that several times, but the word of His power has stopped it, and until He says 'Now— *go!*' it will not go. He upholds "all things by the word of his power".

May we go as far as to say that this should be of personal comfort to us? Sometimes it seems that our own little world is going to pieces, and that we have come to the end. Well, it applies there. He will hold things together until He wants them to go to pieces.

This is the Son identified and described.

And then we move on into the larger body of the Letter: the Son's greatness by comparison with other great things and people. In verse four of the first chapter it says: "*Having become by so much better than the angels*". The angels are the next highest to God and the Son. Oh, there is so much said about angels in the Bible! Peter says that they are great in might and power (II Peter ii. 11). In the book of the Judges an angel is said to have had a very striking appearance, and the person who saw him was afraid she was going to die. She said: "*A man of God came unto me, and his countenance was like the countenance of the angel of God, very terrible*" (Judges xiii. 6).

The angels have a very vast knowledge. Jesus said: "*Of that day and hour knoweth no one, not even the angels of heaven*" (Matthew xxiv. 36). If anyone ought to know, the angels should, for their knowledge is so full and so great, but even the angels do not know this. The angels have a vast knowledge.

There is an overwhelming number of angels: "*The number of them was ten thousand times ten thousand, and thousands of thousands*" (Revelation v. 11). They are a vast number.

The angels are very near to the throne of God, and have access to His Presence. That comes out in one of the most beautiful things that Jesus said about little children— "*See that ye despise not one of these little ones; for I say unto you, that in heaven their angels do always behold the face of my Father which is in heaven*" (Matthew xviii. 10). Of course, we do not understand that, for it is something very mysterious. But Jesus says that the angels have access to the throne of God, and are very near to God Himself. There is only One who is nearer.

The work of the angels is very varied. Look again at this Letter to the Hebrews, because we are keeping very close to it: "*But of which of the angels hath he said at any time, Sit thou on my right hand, till I make thine enemies the footstool of thy feet? Are they not all ministering spirits, sent forth to do service for the sake of them that shall inherit salvation?"* (Hebrews i. 13, 14). And what a lot of work they have to do! Think of all the heirs of salvation, all over the world, in every generation—and this says that the angels have to look after them and their interests! "*To do service for the sake of them that shall inherit salvation.*" Of course, we do not see them, but if the Bible is true the angels are there and are very busy people. They have very much and very valued service. All the various needs of these heirs of salvation are their concern.

So the angels are a very high order—but in this Letter the Lord is saying: 'The Son is far greater than the angels.' It says here, in verse four of the first chapter: "*Having become by so much better than the angels, as he hath inherited a more excellent name than they.*"

If you read all there is about angels in the Bible you will have a very wonderful revelation—and then you come to this fragment about the Son, who is Jesus, "having become by so much better than the angels". That is where the superiority begins.

We have come into the dispensation of that: the superiority of Jesus to all the angels. Perhaps we have not made enough of the ministry of the angels, but they are evidently very busy for us. Possibly we have been saved from many things because they were very watchful.

We begin with the angels—and then we go on with Moses. You will notice what it says in chapter three: "*Wherefore, holy brethren, companions of a heavenly calling, consider the Apostle and High Priest of our confession, even Jesus: who was faithful to him that appointed him, as also was Moses in all his house. For he hath been counted worthy of more glory than Moses*"—(Get hold of that phrase—more honour than Moses!)—"*For every house is builded by some one; but he that built all things is God. And Moses indeed was faithful in all God's house as a servant, for a testimony of those things which were afterward to be spoken; but Christ as a son over God's house"* (Hebrews iii. 1-6— R.V. margin). The writer is saying: 'We are not going to take anything away from Moses. We give him honour as a great servant of God, but Christ is greater. The Son is greater than Moses.'

Abraham was the father of the nation, but Moses was its builder and constitutor. What a large place Moses had in history! He not only had a very large place in Israel, but he has had a large place in the world. Many of the best legal systems are based upon his economy. Because through Moses it was said "Thou shalt not steal" we have all the police forces in the world, and also because he said "Thou shalt not kill". It would be good if we had a few more forces in relation to some other things that Moses said! But the point is: Moses has come to have a very large place in history. The Jews in Christ's day always appealed to Moses as the final authority in anything. Their charge against Jesus was that He made Himself greater than Moses. They believed, therefore, that there was no one greater than Moses: and the writer of this Letter to the Hebrews says, with great boldness, 'There *is* One greater than Moses. Give Moses all the honour due to him, but the Son is greater than he.'

Then the writer goes on to speak of Aaron, who was the first high priest and thus the representative of the whole priestly system. He was over all the other priests and Levites, over all the sacrifices and over the whole sanctuary. On the Day of Atonement he went alone into the place of the Most Holy. No one but Aaron was allowed then to go into the Holy of holies—and the writer here is saying that the Son is greater than Aaron, far greater. And he tells us why: Aaron died. And anyone who dies can never make anything perfect. When he dies he has to leave something unfinished. So the writer is saying: 'Aaron died. Therefore his work was not perfect. Death cut across it. It was never finished. There had to be a succession of high priests to carry on the work.' There were many more priests and many more sacrifices—all being added to try and make this thing perfect, and chapter nine of this Letter says that they never did make anything perfect. There were many high priests, millions of sacrifices and *rivers* of blood, yet never bringing anything to perfection.

And then the Son came—one High Priest for ever, who "*ever liveth*" (Hebrews vii. 25). Therefore His work will never be cut short. "*Thou art a priest for ever*" (Hebrews vii. 17)—and there, in that wonderful paragraph, Melchizedek comes in, and everyone is wondering who he was. Who was Melchizedek? You can go to the Bible and you will never find the answer, and you certainly will not find it outside the Bible. This mysterious man came in, as it were, from nowhere, and where he went to no one knows. He has not beginning nor end, so far as the record is concerned, and that is taken up as illustrating the Lord Jesus as the High Priest—neither beginning of life nor end of days. He is the eternal High Priest. This High Priest, this greater than Aaron, "*ever liveth* (lives for ever) *to make intercession*".

Then He offered one sacrifice for ever. The high priests had used millions of sacrifices but had never made anything perfect. He, with only one sacrifice, did it. It is done for ever, and He was the sacrifice as well as the priest. As priest He offered Himself without blemish unto God.

If we go on like this you will really begin to believe

that there is something better here—better than Moses and better than Aaron. Do you know why God put these two men together? They were brothers, but they were very different. Yet they had to live together and work together? Why was that, and what was the difference? Moses was the governor, representing government and authority. What came through him was 'Thou shalt and thou shalt not'. Moses governed and exercised authority in Israel. But God is not only like that. Aaron was the man of love and of sympathy. Priesthood means just that—love and sympathy: love for the poor sinner, for the poor sinning world, and sympathy with men. God puts these two things together. It would not do to have all of one. It would never do to have only an autocrat. You must unite with the governor, the authority, a heart of compassion. If you have those two things put together you have a very good Israel.

Here in this letter it is saying that Jesus, the Son, is better than Moses and Aaron. On the one side He can say: "*All authority hath been given unto me in heaven and on earth*" (Matthew xxviii. 18). The Father said: "*Sit thou on my right hand, till I make thine enemies the footstool of thy feet*" (Hebrews i. 13).

There are two wonderful pictures in this Letter. The one is of Jesus "crowned with glory and honour", having "sat down on the right hand of the Majesty on high" waiting until His enemies are made 'the footstool of His feet', with all authority in His Power. He is in the place of government. And alongside of that is this other beautiful picture: "For we have not a high priest that cannot be touched with the feeling of our infirmities" (Hebrews iv. 15). . . . "He ever liveth to make intercession for us." Not only authority and government, but love and sympathy—and so much greater than Moses

and Aaron. His authority is a greater authority than that
of Moses, and His government is a greater one than ever
Moses exercised, but His love and sympathy are far
greater than that of Aaron.

I am afraid that this is where we have to stop, though
I have not finished with the superiority of the Son. We
have not touched upon His work—the work of making
purification for sin, but you can read it. Perhaps this is
just like a window opened into heaven. If you get the
right window you can see quite a lot. You can see great
things and you can see far things. But the best that I can
hope is that this has just opened a window, and that as
you look through it you are seeing one thing—how
superior is Jesus Christ to all else, and how superior is the
dispensation into which we have come, and how superior
are all the resources at our disposal to all that ever was
before!

CHAPTER ELEVEN

THE COMPANIONS AS THE BRIDE OF THE LORD

(EARLIER WE SAID that we should be dealing with the Bride more fully later. We come now to a consideration of this matter.)

"*For thy Maker is thine husband; the Lord of hosts is his name: and the Holy One of Israel is thy redeemer*" (Isaiah liv. 5).

"*For as a young man marrieth a virgin, so shall thy sons marry thee: and as the bridegroom rejoiceth over the bride, so shall thy God rejoice over thee*" (Isaiah lxii. 5).

"*Return, O backsliding children, saith the Lord; for I am a husband unto you*" (Jeremiah iii. 14).

"*Behold, the days come, saith the Lord, that I will make a new covenant with the house of Israel, and with the house of Judah: not according to the covenant that I made with their fathers in the day that I took them by the hand to bring them out of the land of Egypt; which my covenant they brake, although I was an husband unto them, saith the Lord*" (Jeremiah xxxi. 31, 32).

"*Judah hath dealt treacherously, and an abomination is committed in Israel and in Jerusalem; for Judah hath profaned the holiness of the Lord which he loveth, and hath married the daughter of a strange god*" (Malachi ii. 11).

That is how the Old Testament finishes. Now we will see how the New Testament finishes.

"Let us rejoice and be exceeding glad, and let us give the glory unto him: for the marriage of the Lamb is come, and his wife hath made herself ready" (Revelation xix. 7).

"And I saw the holy city, new Jerusalem, coming down out of heaven from God, made ready as a bride adorned for her husband" (Revelation xxi. 2).

Revelation xxi. 9–xxii. 21.

[We have been seeing what God is doing particularly in the dispensation in which we live. He is constituting a new, heavenly, spiritual Israel. We have seen the failure of the old Israel and the necessity for God to set it aside, but, at the same time, the bringing in of His new heavenly Israel. This is what is called the 'heavenly calling', and we are told that we are called to be 'companions of the heavenly calling', and 'companions of Christ in the heavenly calling'.

We have seen how the New Testament takes over the ideas of the Old Testament and translates them into spiritual meaning. The titles of the old Israel are redeemed and brought over to the new, because, although God may have to give up an instrument that He raises up, He never gives up His thought. He will never give up His intention, and if He cannot realize His purpose in one instrument, He will do so in another.

We have seen that the old Israel was called 'God's family', the 'Lord's house', 'God's heir for His inheritance', 'God's flock'—they were God's sheep—and all these titles are taken up and brought into the New Testament Church. The new heavenly Israel is God's family, God's children, God's house—*"Whose house are we"* (Hebrews iii. 6)—*"Heirs of God and joint-heirs with Christ"* (Romans viii. 17), God's flock—*"I am the good shepherd"* (John x. 11).]

Well, now we come to a little fuller consideration of the Bride.

Israel, as we have seen from those various Scriptures, was called God's bride. It says that He was a husband to Israel. You will notice that although Israel was a man literally, it is very often spoken of in the feminine. It is not 'he' but 'she', and it was 'she' who failed God as a wife. He purchased Israel with precious blood to be His bride. We have seen that the Passover was a marriage covenant, and Jeremiah, in chapter xxxi, says that when God brought Israel out of Egypt, He took her by the hand and became a husband to her. The blood of the Passover lamb was the blood of a covenant of marriage between the Lord and Israel. He betrothed Israel unto Himself that night, and thus she was purchased with His blood.

Very little need be said to those who know the Old Testament about God's love for Israel. It is the most amazing thing in history. When you think of what Israel was, and read the history of those people from their own side, it is the most wonderful thing to hear the Lord saying: "*I have loved thee with an everlasting love*" (Jeremiah xxxi. 3). God has never given up that love—it is still an everlasting love, but there is a sob in the heart of God. It is a disappointed love.

However, the Old Testament is a wonderful revelation of God's love for Israel: the love of the whole heart of God for a bride. How that love was expressed! See the wonderful protection that the Lord provided for Israel! He protected her all the way along. He provided food and raiment and it says that He led her safely. The tender, providing, protecting love of God is everywhere in the Old Testament.

What was God's thought and intention in betrothing Israel unto Himself? It was that she might be to His

pleasure. The Lord took pleasure in Israel, had brought
her into being for His own pleasure, to bring satisfaction
to His own heart.

Of course, it is a deep mystery why the all-sufficient
God should want something for His pleasure. He who
possessed all things and really had need of nothing is
nevertheless revealed as One who created a people for
His pleasure. You see, He created all things for His
pleasure. He created the world for His pleasure. He
created all that is good in the world for His pleasure. He
created man for His pleasure. And all that went away
from Him. He was disappointed in it all, so He said: 'I
will begin again', and He raised up Israel. His idea was
that Israel would satisfy Him where everything else had
disappointed Him. The bride was for the Bridegroom's
pleasure.

Then, again, Israel was raised up to be the self-revelation of the Lord. God intended to reveal Himself to the
whole universe through Israel, to show what kind of
a husband He is. Of course, we cannot bring this down
to everyday life now, but sometimes you are able to see
by the wife herself what kind of husband she has. As
you look at her, see how she is provided for and cared for,
you are able to say: 'She must have a wonderful husband!'
Well, that is what a wife is for!

The divine thought is just that. God wanted to reveal
to this whole universe what a wonderful God He is in
terms of a husband to Israel. Israel has been raised up, in
New Testament language, to *"show forth the excellencies
of him who called (her) out of darkness into his marvellous
light"* (I Peter ii. 9).

Then Israel was brought into this relationship of the
wife of the Lord for the purpose of His increase, His
expansion. So to speak, many others outside Israel were

to be born unto the Lord through Israel. His family was to expand by means of Israel: *"Nations shall come to thy light, and kings to the brightness of thy rising"* (Isaiah lx. 3). Nations were to be born unto the Lord, and the bride was to be for the Lord's own expansion. These were the things that the prophets said.

Then, last of all—mystery of mysteries!—it was a matter of companionship. None of us can understand why the Lord wanted a companion. It is possible to be a wife and not be a companion. Many a wife is not a real companion to her husband. He does not find her a companion. She is a lot of things, but just that one thing is lacking—real companionship. Perhaps that is the reason for the tragedy of so many broken marriages today. (Of course, it works the other way as well, but companionship is the highest thought in this relationship.) The Lord raised up Israel to be His companion.

It is easy to see how Israel failed in all these matters. The time came when the Lord could no longer take pleasure in her, when she no longer revealed to the world what kind of God He is but turned to other gods, and refused to fulfil the world mission for which she had been brought into union with God. All this resulted in God losing His companion, and the Old Testament closes on that painful note. A horrible thing has happened in Israel. She has left the Lord, her Husband, and gone after 'other lovers'.

So, to the Lord, Israel died. As a nation she is dead to the Lord, "dead while she liveth". The Lord could never marry another while she was alive; that was contrary to His own law. She died, so He could take another wife. You will remember Paul's own words about this: that we are married to the Lord. When this former bride died, God brought in another, a new bride.

The New Testament has a lot to say, as you know, about this new bride. The Lord Jesus in the Gospels calls Himself the Bridegroom. You will remember the parable of the virgins, when the cry went forth: "*Behold, the bridegroom!*" (Matthew xxv. 6). Then we have read these passages in the Book of Revelation about the bride, the Lamb's wife. Some of you are recalling Paul's words in his Letter to the Ephesians: "Christ also loved the church and gave himself up for *her*, that he might sanctify her . . . that he might present the church to himself a glorious church, not having spot or wrinkle or any such thing" (Ephesians v. 25, 27), and that follows this: "Husbands, love your wives, even as Christ also loved the church . . .".

Well, I think the fact is established, but we have to bring back all those features of this relationship. Why are we joined to the Lord? Why are we what are called Christians? For if we are New Testament Christians we are joined to the Lord in a covenant of marriage. It is "*the Church of God, which he purchased with his own Blood*" (Acts xx. 28).

How many of you go to the Lord's Table at any time? It goes by different names—the Lord's Table, the Lord's Supper, the Holy Communion, and so on. It does not matter so much what you call it, but what you mean by it. Do you know that every time you go to the Lord's Table, His meaning in that is that you are putting your hand to the covenant again and are saying: 'I stand by my marriage relationship to the Lord. This loaf means that I am one flesh with Christ.' We are one body in Him, and His very Body is represented by that loaf. The marriage ordinance of God at the beginning was: "*They shall be one flesh*" (Genesis ii. 24). Jesus said: "*This (loaf) is my body*" (Matthew xxvi. 26). When we take the loaf we are *meant* to be saying: 'I am one body with Christ.' It is the marriage relationship.

When we take the cup, symbolic of His Blood, we say two things: 'I share one life with Him. His life is my life, and that was made by a covenant in His Blood.' That is the deep meaning of the Table of the Lord. Is that what we mean every time we go to it? It is the bride saying: 'I stand by the covenant, I am one with my Lord.'

We often sing: "Jesus, my Shepherd, *Husband*, Friend", and that is the nature of our union with Him. That is really what it means to be a Christian. May our Christianity be redeemed from anything less than that!

But when the relationship has been established in His Blood, then its purpose begins. We are His for His pleasure and not our own. He has made us for His pleasure: "*Working in us that which is well-pleasing in his sight*" (Hebrews xiii. 21) . . . "*To the end that we should be unto the praise of his glory*" (Ephesians i. 12) . . . "*that ye may shew forth the excellencies of* him" (I Peter ii. 9).

This compasses the Christian life. This is why He has drawn us with the bands of love and the reason for our union with Christ: that we should be unto *His* pleasure, that He may take pleasure in us. The time is coming when He will look at His bride and then He will say 'She is a glorious bride'. He has brought us to Himself for that very purpose: to reveal Himself by means of us.

Perhaps our heads and our hearts are going down now. What a poor revelation we are of our Lord! We are making a terrible mess of this business of revealing Christ, but He is taking great pains with us. Truly it is not easy, and He does not make it so. It seems that so often He puts us into difficult positions in order that we may show forth His glory.

Paul was given "*a thorn in the flesh, a messenger of Satan*

to buffet me" (II Corinthians xii. 7). Do you know what
it is to have a thorn in the flesh and a messenger of Satan
always buffeting you? Paul says that He went to the Lord
three times about this. I do not know whether he meant
literally three times, but I think he meant: 'I went to the
Lord again, and again, and *again*! I asked the Lord to
remove this thorn and to destroy this messenger of
Satan, but he said unto me: "*My grace is sufficient for thee:
for my power is made perfect in weakness*" (II Corinthians
xii. 9).'

That is strange sovereignty and providence of God! It
seems that He sometimes puts difficulties into our lives,
and makes it hard for us, and then, in the grace that He
shows, we magnify Him. No one knows what Paul's
'thorn' was. A lot of people have had a guess at it, and
some think they know what it was, but I do not think
anyone really does know. It was evidently something that
people could see, and they would say: 'My word, Paul
has a hard time with that. I am very glad the Lord has
not called me to go that way! That poor man does know
what suffering means, but how marvellous is the grace
of God in him! Look at his victorious spirit! My, the
grace of God in that man is a wonderful thing!' And
Paul says: "*And they glorified God in me*" (Galatians i. 24).
Yes, for the self-revelation of the Lord the Church is a
suffering Church. This wife of the Lord is a suffering
wife, but the revelation of His grace is a wonderful
thing.

Then what about His increase through the Church?
We have already said much about this. The Lord, through
His Church, wants to bring many, many into the
Kingdom. Paul said: "*The gospel . . . which was preached
in all creation under heaven*" (Colossians i. 23), and Peter
said: "*The Lord . . . not wishing that any should perish, but*

that all should come to repentance" (II Peter iii. 9). The
Lord would have *all* men saved, and He has never told
His Church to go and pick out one here and one there
and say: 'You are the elect. Come out and leave the
others.' No, He said: 'Preach the Gospel in all the
nations.' Leave the rest with Him!

That is the world mission of the new Israel. But do not
just view it in a general way. Get down to it tomorrow
morning and make this your personal business: to see if
by any means you may be able to bring souls into the
Kingdom.

When we have said all that, we come to this supreme
thing: He has joined us to Himself to be His companions.
That has been our note right through. *"We are become
companions of Christ"* . . . *"Wherefore, holy brethren,
companions of a heavenly calling."*

I confess that I do not understand this: that the Lord
should want us as His friends, not just officially related
to Him, but related to Him as friends. To be a friend of
the Lord! I can only say to you: Let us take that word and
continually ask ourselves 'How would a friend act in
this matter? How would a friend decide? I am called to
be the Lord's friend. I must not fail Him in friendship.
I must not let Him down. He counts upon me to be His
friend.' That is the highest and most sacred part of the
whole relationship.

I despair of ever getting over to you what I see in this
matter! After all this time, I have not yet touched upon
the new Jerusalem! It is a very significant thing that the
new Jerusalem is called 'a bride'. The angel said to John:
*"Come hither, I will shew thee the bride, the wife of the
Lamb"*, and John might have said: 'Now, let us go and
see this wonderful woman.' . . . *"And (he) shewed me the
holy city Jerusalem, coming down out of heaven from God."*

The bride is the city, and the city is the bride. And then you have to read the whole description of the city in Revelation xxi and xxii in order to know what the bride is going to be like. See all the precious stones! This is the preciousness of the Lord Jesus in manifold expression. Peter said: *"For you therefore which believe is the precious-ness"* (I Peter ii. 7). There are *"all manner of precious stones."* It is what Jesus is in His real character revealed in the bride, the city.

Stop thinking about a literal city. This is all a symbolic representation of Christ's bride. All these glories of the city are only the glories of Christ expressed at last in His bride. *"He shewed me the holy city Jerusalem, coming down out of heaven from God, having the glory of God: her light was like unto a stone most precious."* It was shining through all these gems.

All this is what was meant by the Apostle when he said: *"That he might present the church to himself a glorious church"* . . . *"a glorious church"*. The city is the revelation of His manifold glories, and the city is the bride.

Now I have only to close with this final word. These are all very beautiful and wonderful ideas. They are glorious thoughts, but it is just unto this that the Lord has called us. This is the heavenly calling. It is unto this that He wants us to be companions: 'Companions of a heavenly calling' because 'Companions of Christ'.

One hesitates to strike a note that might sound a bit depressing, but be reminded that this great Letter to the Hebrews has many 'ifs' in it. *"Whose house are we, if we hold fast our boldness"* (Hebrews iii. 6) . . . *"We are become companions of Christ if we hold fast"*. This Letter is just full of warnings and strong exhortations, and I do not believe that it was written to non-Christians. All the evidences in it are that it was written to *true* Christians. Therefore, it was saying to them: 'Don't miss your inheritance. Don't fail of your heavenly calling. Do not fail to be true companions of Christ. Do not accept anything less than God's best and His highest.' You can be Christians having much less than God intended. You notice that when the description of the city has been given, it says: *"Blessed are they . . . that may have the right to come in"* (Revelation xxii. 14). There are nations that will not get in. They will walk in the light thereof, but will not be inside. Make sure that you are of this bride. Do not fail the Lord as Israel failed Him.

"Let us . . . press on to full growth" (Hebrews vi. 1— R.V. margin).

Volume 2

THE GREAT TRANSITION
AS INHERENT IN THE GOSPEL BY JOHN

PREFACE

IN Vol. I we have considered the comprehensive presentation of this transition as contained in the Letter to the Hebrews. In this second volume we are taking note of the concentration of that transition as in the Gospel by John. This "Gospel" has been expounded in many ways, mainly in relation to certain specific subjects, as contained in the separate chapters. This method has provided an immense amount of helpful instruction. But the Gospel has rarely—if ever—been shown to have *one* matter governing it from beginning to end. Our object here is to do this and to show that there is one comprehensive issue lying behind the whole. Our method is to indicate this by some sixteen particular connections in the narrative. There are, however, more than sixteen. The messages having been given in conference, the number of meetings only allowed for what is here presented. The spoken form is retained.

T. AUSTIN-SPARKS.

FOREST HILL,
LONDON
1964

CONTENTS

CHAPTER ONE

CHAPTER TWO

CHAPTER THREE

CHAPTER FOUR

CHAPTER ONE

LET ME REMIND you of the all-governing truth which we are considering—that is, what God is doing in this dispensation in which we live. We must be completely clear as to what it is that God is particularly concerned with at this time in the world's history, and, therefore, what it is that we who are the Lord's children are called unto.

The thing that God is doing in this dispensation is the formation of a spiritual and heavenly Israel. In doing that He is repeating the laws of the old Israel *in a spiritual way*. He is following along the lines of His ways with the old Israel, but now *on a heavenly and not an earthly basis*, because, while God's methods may change, His principles are changeless. He has left the earthly basis of the Old Testament and has moved on to a heavenly basis in the New Testament. He has moved from the temporal to the spiritual, and the spiritual is far greater than the temporal.

We are now going to see this in the Gospel by John. This Gospel is all one with the Letter to the Hebrews, because it is just a part of the whole thing that the New Testament represents. It is the embodiment of this matter of the spiritual Israel in a very wonderful way. There are two things that are so clear in this Gospel: one is the Jewish background of the Gospel and the other is the spiritual background behind the Jewish. That spiritual background is in this Gospel being brought to the front and is being made the ground for the whole new dispensation.

Let us look at this. There are at least sixteen marks of the Jewish background in this Gospel by John.

Before moving on to a consideration of these, let us note again that the introduction is a presentation of God's Son. He stands right at the door in the new movement of God toward the heavenly Israel. We are all familiar with this wonderful presentation of Him at the beginning of the Gospel: "*In the beginning was the Word, and the Word was with God, and the Word was God. The same was in the beginning with God. All things were made by him; and without him was not anything made that hath been made*" . . . and there is much more than that, as you can see.

Corresponding to that is the introduction to 'Hebrews': "*God, having of old time spoken unto the fathers in the prophets by divers portions and in divers manners, hath at the end of these days spoken unto us in his Son, whom he appointed heir of all things, through whom also he made the worlds; who being the effulgence of his glory, and the very image of his substance, and upholding all things by the word of his power, when he had made purification of sins, sat down on the right hand of the Majesty on high.*"

The point is that God has founded the dispensation upon His Son and He is the governing factor in it.

Now we go on to what we have called the 'Jewish background of Christ'.

(i) *The Foundation of All—the Lamb of God*

"*On the morrow he seeth Jesus coming unto him, and saith, Behold, the Lamb of God, which taketh away the sin of the world! . . . And he looked upon Jesus as he walked and saith, Behold, the Lamb of God!*" (John i. 29, 36).

We know that the whole Jewish system was built around the Passover lamb. It was the very basis of everything in Israel: the constitution of them as a nation and the greatest governmental factor in all their history. It would be impossible to count the lambs that were offered in Israel through those many centuries. There would have been many millions of lambs slain and rivers of blood from them all!

John sees Jesus and says 'The Lamb!' 'This is God's Lamb!' "Behold, the Lamb of God!" Thus he distinguishes Jesus, marking Him out as the unique Lamb, the one toward whom all the millions of lambs had ever pointed. And just as the Passover lamb was the foundation of the old earthly Israel's life, so we know that this Lamb of God is the very foundation of our whole Christian life. He is the foundation of this dispensation. In the upper room in Jerusalem, on that Passover night, Jesus laid the foundation of the Church for this dispensation, and, while there are other features of the Church's life, the central one is the Table of the Lord. Everything centres in that Table, gathers around it and issues from it. If you had gone into any assembly of the Lord's people in any part of the world in New Testament times, you might have found different things in the different assemblies, but you would have found one thing that was the same in them all, and that was the Lord's Table: the Lamb of God at the centre of everything.

We only make the statement, and note that, right from the beginning, God takes up the figure of the old and makes it the spiritual reality of the new. That which was earthly and temporal in the old Israel is now heavenly and spiritual in the new Israel.

That is the first thing about the Jewish background leading to the heavenly foreground.

(ii) *The Closed and the Opened Heaven*

Reading: John i. 43-51

Do you need to have it pointed out to you that there is quite a lot of Jewish Old Testament in that section? "Moses and the prophets" (verse 45), Jacob and his ladder (verse 51)—they are all there. But Jesus is saying: 'There is a transition from that old to a new, and that is in Myself. Moses and the prophets spoke of Me and the new Israel is centred in Me—an Israel which is not the Jacob in whom there was guile.'

However, the really deep thought and truth in this part concerns the closed and the opened Heaven.

When Jesus said to Nathanael: "*Ye shall see the heaven opened*", He was pointing to an entirely new dispensation. The one characteristic of the Old Testament Jewish system was a closed Heaven. You know that in the old dispensation it was on pain of death that any man came into the presence of God. What a terrible place was that mountain where God was! There were thunders, lightnings and earthquakes, and even Moses said: "*I exceedingly fear and quake*" (Hebrews xii. 21). So terrible was the sound that the people dared not draw near, and if a beast touched the mountain it had to die. During the whole of that dispensation it was 'Keep out! Do not come here where God is, or you will die!' Jacob said: "*I have seen God face to face, and my life is preserved*" (Genesis xxxii. 30), meaning that it was something unusual. It was a closed Heaven and there was no way for the people into the presence of God. Everything said 'Stay out!' and the people knew it. It was a terrible thing to come into the presence of God, for it just meant death. The High Priest had to have very special provision to go into the most holy place, and when God made that provision He said: 'Lest he die'. The Jewish system was a system of judgment and death, of the closed Heaven. There was no way through for man.

But Jesus says: 'You shall see the Heaven opened, and a way between Heaven and earth, between God and man, made clear. I am that way. I will open Heaven by My own blood.' Therefore we can come to Him "*by the blood of Jesus, by the way which he dedicated for us, a new and living way*" (Hebrews x. 20). Jesus said: "*I am the way . . . no one cometh unto the Father, but by me*" (John xiv. 6).

So the second Jewish feature is a closed Heaven, and the second feature of the new Israel is an opened Heaven. And we are enjoying that! We do not stand outside in fear and trembling, wondering whether, peradventure, we dare draw nigh. We can come "*with boldness unto the throne of grace*" (Hebrews iv. 16). Oh, this new dispensation is a better one! This new Israel has privileges which the old one never had.

That is what God is doing in this dispensation, and He has done it in His Son, so that many, many who have been shut out are now finding their way in. God has provided in His Son an opened way for all.

(iii) *The Marriage Failure and Resurrection*

Reading: John ii. 1-11

(Note in verse seven: "Jesus, *knowing in his heart that the Father's time had come* . . .". That was a very important factor for, remember, Jesus would never move on any ground whatsoever without the knowledge that His Father wanted Him to move. He waited for that. When He knew in His heart that the Father said 'Yes, go on', "*Jesus saith unto them, Fill the waterpots with water*".)

Now where is the Jewish background? We have said

that the Lord's Table was, amongst other things, the time when the Lord instituted His marriage with His people. In the Old Testament a marriage covenant was made in the Passover. Jeremiah spoke of this when he said: *"the day that I took them by the hand . . . I was an husband unto them, saith the Lord"* (Jeremiah xxxi. 32), and that was on the Passover night.

Jesus knew what He was doing at Cana. How many times we have heard people talk about Him being of a social disposition and, therefore, He was quite happy to attend marriages! That might be true, but it is not the meaning here. Jesus was always acting on spiritual grounds. The marriage between God and Israel had broken down, for Israel had violated the terms of the covenant of marriage with Jehovah. They had, as the prophets said, become an adulterous nation and had gone after other gods. Therefore the marriage had broken down. That is here, in figure, in Cana.

I don't know what was behind this, but we can judge from a lot of other things that God was behind the failure of the wine. It just *had* to fail because of the spiritual significance. It represented the old marriage relationship which had broken down, had come to an end. There had to be a new basis and a new marriage supper of the Lamb. The salvation of the marriage relationship between God and His people is in Jesus only. It was He who saved the situation here, and everyone knew that something very wonderful and super-natural had happened. It was not natural or earthly. It was heavenly, spiritual, super-natural, and so is that marriage relationship between Christ and His people.

There is a movement from the old Israel, which has failed and has been put aside, to a new Israel which lives by this life of Jesus Christ.

(iv) *The Temple of God—Temporal and Spiritual*

Reading: John ii. 13-22

There is no need to point out the Jewish background! It had the temple in Jerusalem as its centre. For the Jews that temple represented everything—and Jesus speaks of the destroying of the temple! In another place He said: *"There shall not be left here one stone upon another"* (Matthew xxiv. 2).

Well, what is going to take its place? God *must* have a temple! Jesus said, in effect, 'I am the temple of the new dispensation. I am going to take the place of this old temple and I am going to be *all* that that temple represented, but in a fuller and better way.' Was the temple the place where men thought that they would meet God? Men will meet God in Christ in a more real way than that. Was the temple the place to which people went to be taught about God? They will learn more about God in Christ than they ever learned in that temple. Was the temple the place where men went to worship God? It will be in Christ that men will come into touch with God for worship.

And that leads us to that wonderful revelation which we have in the New Testament—the revelation of Christ and all His members being made one temple for God.

Christ is our Temple, and in Him we find all that a temple was ever intended to be. Oh, how people have gone astray over this! We go to many places that are called 'churches' and the word is applied to the building. When people pray in those places they usually say something like this: 'We have come into Thy house today. We are in this house of God.' They are really talking about a building. But we don't need a building to give God a temple! *"Where two or three are gathered*

together in my name, there am I in the midst of them"
(Matthew xviii. 20). People gathered into Jesus Christ
constitute the temple of God. It is not a special building,
but people who are in Christ Jesus. This is what God is
doing in this dispensation.

You know, a lot of people have lost their special
buildings, or are not allowed to meet in such places. In
some places they are gathering in twos and threes and
are enjoying all the privileges of the house of God
because the Lord is there. No, the temple now is Christ
and those who are in union with Him. So He said, in
this way which they did not understand, "*Destroy this
temple, and in three days I will raise it up*". Christ in
resurrection is the temple of this dispensation. He knew
that He was speaking parabolically and what they would
say: "*Forty and six years was this temple in building*". It
looked as though He had deliberately misled them, but
He was enunciating the change of dispensations.

(v) *The True Seed of Abraham*

Reading: John iii. 1-14

What have we here in Nicodemus? Surely he is a
representative of the old Israel! He is of the sect of the
Pharisees and they claimed to be very representative of
Israel. He is a ruler of the Jews, so he is indeed Israel in
representation. He is a son of Abraham after the flesh,
the embodiment of the seed of Abraham.

What does the Lord Jesus say to him? In effect, He
says: 'You, a son of Abraham, an inclusive representation
of the children of Abraham after the flesh, an embodiment
of Israel, I look upon you, Nicodemus, as representing all
the seed of Abraham after the flesh, as all Israel present
here tonight in you, and you, Nicodemus, in that

representative capacity, must be born again.' The seed of Abraham after the flesh does not stand in the Kingdom of God.

You know, that is Paul's argument in his Letters to the Romans and the Galatians. He says they are not all Israel which are after Israel. There is a natural seed and there is a spiritual seed.

Jesus was saying to Nicodemus, in his representative capacity: 'The natural seed of Abraham does not stand. Israel after the flesh is no more. You must be born again. There must be a seed after the Spirit. In other words, there must be a new spiritual, heavenly Israel. *"That which is born of the flesh is flesh"* and *"They that are in the flesh cannot please God"* (Romans viii. 8). *"That which is born of the Spirit is spirit. Marvel not that I said unto thee, Ye must be born anew".'*

The new Israel of this dispensation is the Israel of the 'born from above' ones. These are not the sons of Abraham, but sons of God.

And so we are back in chapter one: *"As many as received him, to them gave he the right to become children of God."* There is a great deal of difference between children of Abraham after the flesh and children of God after the Spirit! And not only a great deal of difference: it is not just an improved species. It is an altogether higher race, a heavenly people.

CHAPTER TWO

(vi) The Serpent, the Curse: Jesus Lifted Up

"And as Moses lifted up the serpent in the wilderness, even so must the Son of man be lifted up: that whosoever believeth may in him have eternal life" (John iii. 14, 15).

Here is the Old Testament background, which we have in the twenty-first chapter of the Book of Numbers. There the incident begins in this way: *"The people spake against God, and against Moses . . . our soul loatheth this vile bread"* (Numbers xxi. 5—R.V. margin). They used very strong words about the manna, the food from heaven. They spoke against God and Moses and said: 'We hate the thing God has provided.'

Do remember that God, in all that He did, always had His Son in view, and this was so when He gave the children of Israel the manna from heaven (as we shall see when we come to John vi). The manna was a type of Christ, who said: *"The bread of God is that which cometh down out of heaven, and giveth life unto the world . . . I am the bread of life"* (John vi. 33, 35). The people of Israel said: 'We loathe this vile bread' . . . and you can hear the Jews in Christ's day speaking like that: 'We hate this man!' That was their spirit.

God saw the spirit of these people in the wilderness. How antagonistic it was to Him and to what He gave! Therefore *"the Lord sent fiery serpents among the people, and they bit the people; and much people of Israel died"* (Numbers

xxi. 6). "*And as Moses lifted up the serpent in the wilderness, even so must the Son of Man be lifted up.*"

Oh, there are deep and terrible things here! From the beginning to the end of the Bible the serpent is ever and always the symbol of a curse, of the judgment of God. You know that from the very first mention of the serpent in the Bible. This serpent lifted up in the wilderness was the symbol of the judgment of God. The judgment and curse of God which rested upon the rebellious people were transferred to that serpent. It was transfixed to the cross, carrying the curse and the judgment of God upon itself for the people, and whosoever looked to the serpent was saved.

In using that bit of the Old Testament, the Lord Jesus was only saying: 'I am going to be made a curse for you. When I am lifted up I shall bear *your* judgment upon Myself. I shall carry *your* sins in My body on the tree.' There is deliverance in Christ crucified from the curse and from the judgment, and whosoever will look shall live. And here comes in the greatest Scripture that we know! "*For*" (I like the conjunction. Conjunctions are always significant things in the New Testament. When you get a 'for', 'wherefore' or 'therefore', always look all round) "*God so loved the world.*"

We so often quote John iii. 16 without the context. Ah, what a tremendous thing this is! God has laid on His only-begotten Son the iniquity of us all, allowing Him, His well-beloved Son, to be made a curse for us. Why? "*For God so loved the world, that he gave his only begotten Son, that whosoever believeth on him should not perish, but have eternal life.*" You have to lift that out and put it right into Numbers xxi, or take Numbers xxi and put it right into John iii. 16.

Here is the background and here is the foreground, the

transition from the old to the new. The new heavenly Israel is built upon this ground: "*Whosoever believeth may in him have eternal life.*"

What a lot more we could say about that! But we must pass on.

(vii) *The Opened Way to the Springing Well*

(Here is another unfortunate dividing of chapters. For spiritual purposes it is a great pity that John iii and John iv are divided.)

Reading: John iv. 1-42

The heart of the whole talk between the Master and the woman of Samaria is in verse 14:

"*Whosoever drinketh of the water that I shall give him shall never thirst; but the water that I shall give him shall become in him a well of water springing up unto eternal life.*"

1 have just said that there ought to be no division of chapters here, because the twenty-first chapter of the Book of Numbers is not divided. Immediately after the incident of the serpent being lifted up there comes the incident of the springing well: "*Then sang Israel this song: Spring up, O well:*" (Numbers xxi. 17). When the Cross has done its work, when Christ has borne the judgment and the curse resting upon us, then the Holy Spirit is released and springs up as the well of eternal life.

There, then, in chapter four is the background of Numbers xxi—the springing well following immediately upon the serpent being lifted up. In John iii and iv you have these two things: Jesus lifted up, being made a curse for us (for it is written: "*He that is hanged is accursed of God*" (Deuteronomy xxi. 23)), and bearing the judgment of our rebellious hearts. Then, when He has done that, He has made a way for the springing well of eternal life.

The Holy Spirit makes a wonderful connection in the Bible, does He not? How He brings things together! We would, perhaps, have never thought of finding the third and fourth chapters of John in the twenty-first chapter of Numbers, but there they are.

(viii) *The Word of Life and the Law of Death*

Reading: John iv. 46-54

Here we have the incident of the nobleman and his dying son. He has come all the way from Capernaum to find Jesus and to persuade Him to go home with him and heal his son. Jesus tested his faith, and, finding that it was quite genuine, said: "*Go thy way. Thy son liveth.*" The man believed Him, went home and discovered that it was just at the very moment that Jesus said: "Thy son liveth" that the boy began to get better.

What is at the heart of this incident? Why did Jesus not go to Capernaum with that man? He went there on another occasion and healed a lot of people. Why did He not say: 'Well, I have to return to Capernaum at some time and do a lot of works there. I may as well go now. Here is the opportunity. It is an invitation and I suppose I ought to take all invitations'?

Jesus did not do that. He stayed where He was and sent the man home all those miles. It took from twelve noon until the close of that day, and then on into the next day, for the man to get home. Why was it that Jesus adopted this method on this particular occasion?

We have a Jewish background. What is it? It is the background of the law: "*The letter killeth*" (II Corinthians iii. 6). Jesus said: "*The words that I have spoken unto*

you are spirit, and are life" (John vi. 63). It does not
matter how far away the case may be, if He speaks His
word is spirit and life.

The Old Testament speaking of the law brought death.
"The letter killeth" (that is, the letter of the law). *"The
spirit giveth life"* (II Corinthians iii. 6) and *"the words that
I have spoken unto you are spirit, and are life."* Jesus had only
to speak and He reversed the effect of the law. The law
could never have done this. You may bring all the
scribes and Pharisees down from Jerusalem to this boy
and they can recite all the law of Moses, and nothing will
happen. He will die right enough, and probably all the
quicker because of their reading of the law! Jesus had
only to open His mouth and speak a word, and the boy
many miles away began to get better from that moment.

Yes, Jesus is saying that the law of His mouth is life.
The transition is so clear—from death unto life in the
Word.

(ix) *The Release from the Bondage to Self*

Reading: John v. 1-9

In this story of the impotent man the heart of the
matter is in verse five: *"And a certain man was there, which
had been thirty and eight years in his infirmity."*

What is the Jewish background? There is very little
doubt that it was Israel's journey in the wilderness, the
thirty-eight years of their wanderings. What cripples
they were! They could have made the journey from
Egypt to Canaan in eleven days, but it took them thirty-
eight years and during that time they were really making
no progress at all. They were in bondage to their own
self-life. They were impotent, helpless cripples because
the self-life was in the place of mastery. You have no

need for me to tell you how that self-life governed them in the wilderness. They never looked at anything in the light of how it served God and how far it satisfied His interests. They looked at everything in the light of how it affected them. All their murmuring and rebellion was because *they* were not getting what *they* wanted. It was never what God wanted. They were just a self-centred people, and the self-life was their bed, and they were cripples lying on that bed. They were never really able to get up and march straight forward into God's purpose.

Well, that is the Jewish background, and Jesus takes up an illustration of that right in the presence of the Jews when He puts this man on his feet.

The members of the new heavenly Israel are people who have been delivered from self-interest into God's interest, who have been put on their spiritual feet by Jesus Christ and are walking in strength in the way of the Lord.

Do you not think it is a very significant thing that the first miracle after the Day of Pentecost was the raising of an impotent man at the gate of the temple in Jerusalem? These are not just pretty stories put together to make an interesting book. God knows what He is doing, and when He makes the first miracle of the Christian era the raising of an impotent cripple, He is saying that the people of this new Israel are people who have been delivered from this impotence and put on their feet spiritually.

There are a lot of Christian cripples about! They cannot get on their own feet, nor can other people put them there. You try to pick them up! They may take a step or two, and then down they go again. There are many like that, and you can spend your life trying to get them up on their feet. What is it that is eating the very life out of them? What is it that is making them such

helpless cripples that they cannot walk? It is self-centred-
ness. Make no mistake about it, it is self in some form.
It is self that wants to be taken notice of. It is self in the
form of pride. This poor man was delivered because he
knew his own helplessness and he believed what Jesus
said. He believed on to Jesus Christ, which means that
he believed out of himself. Yes, that is the secret—that
we shall turn from our miserable selves and cease to be
occupied with them, saying once and for all: 'I am done
with you, wretched self. I throw myself on to Jesus
Christ. I take the one great step of committal.' Jesus
never lets such a person down.

(x) *The Miracle and Mystery of Heavenly Sustenance*

Reading: John vi

We have already said something about this. The
Jewish background comes in verse thirty-two: "*It was
not Moses that gave you the bread out of heaven; but my
Father*".

Right in the presence of the Jews, Jesus is saying: "*The
bread of God is that which cometh down out of heaven, and
giveth life unto the world . . . I am the bread of life*".

With John's extensive context of the manna in the
wilderness covering seventy-one verses there is one issue
which plainly arises. It is the issue of divine sustenance
in humanly impossible conditions. That this matter is
taken out of the natural into the super-natural realm is
clear. Nicodemus—that representative of Israel—had
confronted a demand made by Christ with a mighty
'How?' "*How can a man be born when he is old?*" That
question postulated the miracle of the beginning of the
Christian life. In the chapter now before us the Jews
raised another question: "*How can this man give us his*

flesh to eat?" (verse 52). This question—with the context of the feeding of the multitude in the wilderness—postulates the miracle of the continuance and support of the Christian life in naturally impossible conditions. That Christ Himself as "The Bread of Life" maintains the life of God's people when there is nothing but spiritual desolation all around is, firstly, a miracle; secondly, a fact; and thirdly, a test of the reality of union with Him. This miracle and fact are attested by a long history of the stamina and persistence of so many who have had no *earthly* means of spiritual support. If our life is centred in Christ Himself, and not merely in religious things, it will be a miracle how we go on.

Perhaps this is one of the ways in which the manifold wisdom of God is made known, by the Church, unto principalities and powers, and we are 'unto the glory of His grace'.

(xi) *All Sacrifices and Offerings fulfilled*

Reading: John vii. 1, 2, 14, 37-39

We are here in the presence of the feast of tabernacles, and that goes back to the twenty-ninth chapter of the Book of Numbers. If you look there you will see what led up to this great day of the feast. All the different kinds of offerings had been presented to the Lord (I need not enumerate them—they are all mentioned in the chapter), and then came the last great day of the feast. It is called the 'feast of tabernacles', but it is also called 'the feast of trumpets'. On the last great day the priests brought out great vessels of water and poured it out on the top of the steps of the temple in Jerusalem so that it flowed down in great volume.

Jesus stepped forward at that time. In Him all the

offerings are presented to God. He in person is the
embodiment of all the sacrifices and all the offerings and
He, as the completeness of all God's requirements,
presents Himself to the Lord. Then He comes to this day
of the feast of tabernacles. In Numbers it says: "*It is a day
of blowing of trumpets unto you*". Jesus, so to speak, took
the trumpet and 'cried with a loud voice'. Here, in figure,
is the trumpet of the feast of tabernacles. In Him all the
offerings are perfected. God is fully satisfied and, therefore, He can pour out His Spirit in fulness. Jesus cried
like a trumpet: "*He that believeth on me . . . out of him shall
flow rivers of living water.*"

This is the heritage of all who are of the new Israel. It
is your inheritance. If the Word of God is true, if what
Christ has said is true (and He wanted it to be known that
it was true by crying with a loud voice), and if you and
I will accept Jesus Christ as God's full satisfaction on our
behalf, as the One who has brought every offering that
God has stipulated to God Himself, who has answered
to every sacrifice and every offering, then His great cry
is true for us. Rivers of living water can flow out of us
and others can receive His life through us, who are His
channels. That is how it ought to be with every true
believer, and Jesus has made it possible by satisfying
God completely on our behalf.

So people of the new Israel ought to be people with a
river flowing out of them. Believe, proclaim your faith,
do not be silent, take the trumpet and let people hear, and
you will be surprised that, when you begin to testify to
the Lord Jesus, other people will receive life. Something
will happen to them. If you keep your mouth closed and
refuse to testify to the Lord Jesus in your home, in your
village and in your work, then you are holding up the
river of the Spirit. You are checking the flow of the river

that ought to be flowing out from you.

Now, if you have never done it, you try it! I want to tell you that the first soul who comes to the Lord Jesus through your testimony will release something in you, so that you will never want to keep your mouth closed again. There are a lot of miserable Christians who will keep their mouths closed. I know there are those who talk too much, but there are quite a lot who do not talk enough and so they are spoiling their own Christian life. Take the trumpet of the Lord Jesus and cry with a loud voice and the rivers will begin to flow.

We—the new Israel—must keep the feast of tabernacles by proclaiming the all-sufficiency of Jesus, to God *for* us; *from* God to us!

CHAPTER THREE

(xii) *Human and Religious Blindness, and Heavenly Sight*

Reading: John viii. 12–ix. 41

It is a pity that these chapters are divided, because in chapter nine Jesus is showing the truth of what He has been saying in chapter eight in a very practical way.

It is perfectly clear that this incident is set in the background of the earthly Israel, and this long section of the record is intended to show that Israel after the flesh is blind. If ever men demonstrated how blind they were, these people did in all this argument! Jesus is making them give themselves away. That is, He is just compelling them to betray their own blindness. The fact is that these people were just not seeing. They were spiritually blind, as that man was naturally blind. So that what we have here is set in Israel's blindness, all with the object of showing this specific characteristic of the new spiritual Israel which the Lord Jesus was bringing into being.

Will you retain that for a few minutes, as we are going away from it for a little while—because there is one marvellous truth which embraces all these things which we are saying, and that is that no thought that God has ever expressed dies. There is no lapse of any thought that God has expressed. God expressed His thoughts in the very conception and constitution of the Israel of old. They were in all that was said about Israel and in all that was revealed as to God's purpose in Israel. God expressed His thoughts concerning Israel in a multitude of ways. That Israel failed to answer to the thoughts of God. His thoughts concerning Israel were never fully realized because of their rebellion. So that Israel was passed by, but God's thoughts were not put aside. All those same thoughts are taken up in a new Israel.

Jesus Himself becomes the inclusive new Israel. You remember that when He referred to Jacob, whose name was changed to Israel, He said to Nathanael: "*Ye shall see the heaven opened, and the angels of God ascending and descending upon the Son of man*" (John i. 51). So Jesus is the new Israel in person. All the communications of God and Heaven to man are by way of Jesus, the new Israel. All God's thoughts in the past ages are taken up in the Lord Jesus in the first place. All that was ever intended by God concerning Israel and was lost by them is carried on in the Lord Jesus, and then transferred by Him to His companions and the companions of the heavenly calling —the new Israel, which is spiritual.

This opens up a very big realm for you. It would be impossible to number all the characteristics of God's mind concerning Israel, but let us just indicate what we mean.

You know, God marked Israel off as a people distinct from all other people in appearance. Some years ago, before he went to the Lord, I knew a very distinguished Hebrew Christian. He used to travel all over the world, and he once said this to me: 'Wherever I go, in all parts of the world, I always know when I meet a Jew. They may have lived for generations in this country or in that, but there is something about them that they never lose. I always know they are Jews without being told.' God marked them out as a people distinct from all other races.

Now see how that is taken up in the Lord Jesus and in

His true companions. Whenever you meet a true
Christian in this world, you know it before he or she is
introduced to you. It is not the shape of his or her face,
or, indeed, by any outward form, but there is never any
need for anyone to bring them to you and say: 'This is
a Christian.' You come into their presence and there is
something about them that is different. Then when you
begin to talk you know that you have met one of your
own race. Their outward features may be those of the
Chinese, Indian, British, or anything else, but there are
spiritual features which mark them out as different from
all others: "*They took knowledge of them, that they had
been with Jesus*" (Acts iv. 13).

That is a truth, but we must very sacredly safeguard
that truth. There are far too many who bear the name of
Christ who cannot be distinguished from the world.

However, our point is this: Whatever the expressed
thought of God was, in any one of a thousand ways, if
Israel lost that thought, it is taken up in Jesus Christ and
is transferred by Him to His companions. The companions of Christ always take some of His character.
That is why someone started the name 'Christian': "*The
disciples were called Christians first in Antioch*" (Acts xi. 26).
Someone said: 'These are *Christ ones*.'

That is a very large truth within which we are speaking
in these chapters. Israel was called to be God's instrument
of light to the world. He raised them up to be for Him
light to all the nations. They were all intended to come
to know God through Israel, to see what He was like
and to come into a knowledge of Him. Israel was set in
the nations to be the light of the world. God intended to
reflect Himself on this earth through Israel. It was intended
that the light of God should fall upon Israel like a mirror
and then be reflected from them to shine forth to all the

nations. There were times when it was like that to some extent—but what a tragedy Israel became in that particular! The time came when God was veiled by Israel rather than revealed. Israel became a terrible contradiction of God. When you pick up these Gospels and read all these arguments between Jesus and the leaders of Israel, and all that is in them as to the Jewish rulers, the way they behaved, the way they talked and the spirit that they showed, you say: 'Well, if that were God, I would want to have nothing to do with Him.' That is a terrible misrepresentation of God! And because of that God put Israel aside, but in this particular respect He did not put His thought aside.

At that time, when Israel was about to be rejected, God's Son came into the world, and He took up the thought of God that was intended to be realized in Israel and He said, right in the midst of this dark and blind people, "*I am the light of the world*". 'Israel has failed. I take the place of Israel, and in Me and through Me shall all the world know what God is like.' "While I am in the world *I am the light of the world: he that followeth me shall not walk in the darkness, but shall have the light of life.*" God always intended that the races of this world should have the light of life, life-giving light, liberating light.

"*If therefore the Son shall make you free, ye shall be free indeed.*" How does the Son make us free? "*Ye shall know the truth, and the truth shall make you free*" . . . "*I am the light of the world*", and the effect of the light is to set men free.

Do you remember the commission given by the Lord to the Apostle Paul at the time of his conversion? It is most illuminating and instructive in the light of what we are saying. The Lord said to Paul: "*Unto whom I send thee, to open their eyes, that they may turn from darkness*

to light, and from the power of Satan unto God" (Acts xxvi.
17, 18). He was to be sent to those who were prisoners
of Satan and therefore in the dark, to turn them from
darkness to light and from the power of Satan unto God.
Every member of the human race is by nature in the
devil's prison.

You will remember that in Bunyan's *Holy War* there
is set forth the battle for man's soul, and all the forces
of Apollyon are attacking to capture man's soul, which
is represented as a city. Apollyon calls his leaders together
and says: 'If we are going to capture Mansoul we must
first of all capture the burgomaster. His name is Mr.
Understanding. We must capture him and put him in
a dark dungeon so that he does not see what is happening.'
There is a stroke of genius in that! The Word says:
"Having the understanding darkened" (Ephesians iv. 18—
A.V.). . . . *"The god of this world hath blinded the minds of
the unbelieving that the light of the gospel of the glory of
Christ, who is the image of God, should not dawn upon them"*
(II Corinthians iv. 4). If light comes from Jesus to any
soul, that soul is liberated, and the whole strategy of
Apollyon is upset.

Yes, how important it is to the god of this age to
blind the minds of men and to put Mr. Understanding
in a dark dungeon, thus making sure that he does not
see what is going on!

And that is the state of every child of Adam after the
flesh. The Lord was saying to Israel: 'That is where you
have got to. You, who were intended to be the light of
the world, are now involved in the very darkness of the
world. You are a contradiction of God's thought and
intention.'

That is quite clear and evident, is it not? However, it is
the negative side. We repeat: what Israel failed to realize

is taken up in the person of God's Son and is transferred to the new, collective Israel, called in the Hebrew Letter 'the companions of Christ'.

Do you see what the companions of Christ are supposed to be like? They are supposed to be the very vessels in which this truth is fulfilled. They are supposed to be the very temples of Christ, and in them He is the light: *"Christ in you, the hope of glory"* (Colossians i. 27).

That would lead us to a very large study. You know that the New Testament has a very great deal to say about spiritual understanding, and the tremendous importance of spiritual knowledge. It puts a very high and great value upon this faculty of spiritual sight. You will remember that it says: *"It is God that said, Light shall shine out of darkness, who shined in our hearts, to give the light of the knowledge of the glory of God in the face of Jesus Christ. But we have this treasure in earthen vessels, that the exceeding greatness of the power may be of God, and not from ourselves"* (II Corinthians iv. 6, 7). Do you notice what surrounds that marvellous statement? It is connected with Moses going up into the mountain where God was, receiving the law at the mouth of God, and then coming down the mountain, not knowing that his face was shining. It says: *"Moses wist not that the skin of his face shone"* (Exodus xxxv. 29), but the people saw it and could not look. The light was too strong and they could not look upon the face of Moses, so Moses took a veil and put it over his face and hid the glory of God behind the veil. 'Now', says the Apostle, bringing this right up to date, 'from that time unto now there is a veil upon the heart of Israel. They are incapable of looking upon the glory of God. . . . *"But whensoever it shall turn to the Lord, the veil is taken away. Now the Lord is the Spirit: and where*

C

the Spirit of the Lord is, there is liberty" (II Corinthians
iii. 16, 17).' When the Holy Spirit shines Christ in, there
is liberty. The life is liberated.

Oh, it is wonderful just to see something of the Lord
by the Holy Spirit!

What we have said is the statement of fact, and when
the facts have been stated we are only at the beginning of
the matter. You will never be liberated by a statement of
fact! We may state facts for years, but they will make no
difference. Something has got to happen. It has to begin
to happen if you are not already born again, but what
has to happen at the beginning of your Christian life
is what happened to this man who was born blind: you
have to be able to say exactly the same words that he
used: "*One thing I know, that, whereas I was blind, now
I see.*" 'There are a lot of things that I do not know, but
one thing I *do* know.' That is the characteristic of the
beginning of a true companion of Jesus Christ.

But that is only the beginning of seeing. The Apostle
Paul had given a tremendous amount of teaching to the
believers in Ephesus. He said to them: "*I shrank not from
declaring unto you the whole counsel of God*" (Acts xx. 27).
He spent some years with them and just poured out to
them the light that he had. They were therefore Christians who had a lot of instruction. After that Paul went to
prison and when there he wrote a letter to them, in
which he said: "*Making mention of you in my prayers;
that the God of our Lord Jesus Christ, the Father of glory, may
give unto you a spirit of wisdom and revelation in the knowledge of him, having the eyes of your heart enlightened*"
(Ephesians i. 16-18). That was not for their salvation.
They had been saved a long time and had been taught
very much. They had gone a long way with the Lord—
but Paul still prayed this prayer. In effect he was saying:

'All that you have received and all that I have given you is nothing to what there is yet to see in the Lord Jesus. And for all that you need to have your eyes opened. You need the spirit of wisdom and revelation.' How important this is!

Do you notice how Paul finished that Letter? "*Our wrestling is not against flesh and blood, but against the principalities, against the powers, against the world-rulers of this darkness, against the spiritual hosts of wickedness*" (Ephesians vi. 12). What is it that these are seeking to do? They are trying to rob you of the light. Paul says there: "*Put on the whole armour of God, that ye may be able to stand against the wiles of the devil*" (Ephesians vi. 11). The *wiles* of the devil are, among other things, to stop you getting more light, to rob you of the light that you have, to bring in something that will blind your eyes, and to get them off the Lord Jesus on to something else, perhaps on to yourself, or on to some worldly interest. As soon as that happens you will go into bondage and will be helpless prisoners again. The evil forces are "the world-rulers of *this darkness*" (Ephesians vi. 12).

This matter of spiritual enlightenment is a great battle. Indeed, there is always a battle bound up with receiving more true spiritual light.

We must leave it there for the present, though we have come only to the threshold of a very great matter. We close by repeating what we have already said: This great thought of God is taken up in Christ and transferred to His companions.

We might have said something about Christ's battle with His own companions in the days of His flesh about this matter. He had chosen twelve, the number of the tribes of Israel. He had made them His companions, but, oh, what difficulty He had in making them understand!

He had sometimes to say: 'Do you not yet understand?'
and He had to put His teaching into parables for little
children, to try to get through their dark minds some
understanding of spiritual truth. *"The sower went forth to
sow"*—you know the picture. But it is a picture for little
children, is it not? And He told them all the other
parables. When He had finished them all, He had to tell
the disciples that it was necessary to speak to them like
that because they had no understanding. All the way
through He was battling with their dark minds, and was
pointing on to a day when they would understand.
However, because He knew that day was coming, He did
not give them up. 'In that day ye shall ask Me no more
questions . . . *"When he, the Spirit of truth, is come, he shall
guide you into all the truth"* (John xvi. 13).'

I have often thought that the Lord Jesus must have been
very happy on the Day of Pentecost! Have you read
Peter's address to the multitude on that day? (Here is
a nice little bit of Bible study for you—make a list of all
the subjects included in that address.) It is packed full of
the Old Testament, and Peter is saying: 'Why, it is all
being fulfilled in Jesus Christ!' That is what Jesus
laboured for three and a half years to get them to understand! And on the Day of Pentecost, when the Holy
Spirit had come, why, the Bible was wide open to them.
They saw it all and were set free by the truth and the
light. I think Jesus must have been saying: 'This is what
I lived and suffered for! These men are seeing at last.
They are My companions now.'

The companions of Jesus are those who see as He sees.
How true that is of all companionship! There is really no
companionship between two people if they do not see
alike. You might want to keep together, but, oh! how
difficult it is when one does not see what you see. You

can go so far and no further. The Scriptures say: "*Can two walk together, except they be agreed?*" (Amos iii. 3). Real companionship rests upon mutual understanding, and I think there are few things that Jesus wants and longs for more than to have people who understand Him. This is what God ever wanted, and this thought is taken up in His Son and is passed on to the Son's companions. John says: "*If we walk in the light, as he is in the light, we have fellowship one with another*" (1 John i. 7). Fellowship with the Lord and with one another—if we walk in the light. I dare to say that you have received, at least in word, a good deal of light. All I can say is: Walk in it, and you will be set free.

CHAPTER FOUR

(xiii) *The Shepherd of Israel*

Reading: John x

The heart of this chapter is in verse eleven: "*I am the good shepherd*". Let us put alongside of that the following passages of Scripture:

"*Thou leddest thy people like a flock, by the hand of Moses and Aaron*" (Psalm lxxvii. 20).

"*He led forth his own people like sheep, and guided them in the wilderness like a flock*" (Psalm lxxviii. 52).

"*Take heed unto yourselves, and to all the flock, in the which the Holy Ghost hath made you overseers, to feed the church of God, which he purchased with his own blood. I know that after my departing grievous wolves shall enter in among you, not sparing the flock; and from among your own selves shall men arise, speaking perverse things, to draw away the disciples after them*" (Acts xx. 28-30).

"*Now the God of peace, who brought again from the dead the great shepherd of the sheep with the blood of the eternal covenant, even our Lord Jesus, make you perfect in every good thing to do his will*" (Hebrews xiii. 20, 21).

Here we have the flock spoken of, both in the Old Testament and in the New. There need be no argument about the fact that the Lord looked upon Israel of old as His sheep. The nations were judged by God because of their treatment of His sheep: they destroyed and scattered them. God was very angry with the false shepherds in Israel because they failed to fulfil their trust to the sheep.

There is more, as we have seen, in the Psalms about Israel as the Lord's sheep.

We begin our meditation on this matter by speaking about the Lord as the owner of the sheep. That is the great point which governs this whole matter. The sheep belong to the Lord. They are His, and His ownership of them is emphasized everywhere. The sheep exist for the Shepherd, and the Shepherd exists for the sheep. The love of God for Israel as His sheep is to be noted everywhere. They were *the people of his pasture, and the sheep of his hand*" (Psalm xcv. 7). The love of God for the old Israel was a very wonderful thing. What care He showed for His sheep in the wilderness! How, as a Shepherd, He provided water and pasture for them, even in a desert. How angry He was when anyone touched His sheep! Touch one of His sheep and you touch the Lord! The Lord claimed the ownership of His sheep, and because He owned them and they were His sheep, everything He did was because of that.

In these days we are seeing how God, on the one side, had to forsake Israel. The God who had so loved Israel, had been so jealous for them, had done everything that He could for them, had at last to accept their repudiation of Him as their Shepherd.

Why was that? It was not like God! It seems to be such a contradiction of Him. He would never, never do that if He could possibly avoid it. He had said: "*I have loved thee with an everlasting love*" (Jeremiah xxxi. 3). It was a terrible thing for God to have to forsake Israel, but He *had* to do it. And today Israel is in that condition—no longer God's flock, as in old time. Those sheep are scattered over all the world, without a shepherd.

Why did that come about? Simply for this one reason: Israel's fatal sin was their repudiation of God as their one

Shepherd. They turned to other gods and made them their shepherds. They followed their voices, and repudiated the sole ownership of the Lord. That great chapter, Isaiah liii, shows their attitude toward the Shepherd. A word rises out of that chapter: *"All we like sheep have gone astray"*, and it goes on to show how Israel treated God's provided Shepherd.

It is impressive to note that the Apostle Paul quotes this very thing in his Letter to the Romans: *"But they did not all hearken to the glad tidings. For Isaiah saith, Lord, who hath believed our report?"* (Romans x. 16). Israel refused to believe the message of the prophets, and that message was all about God as the Shepherd and Israel as the sheep. And the prophet says: 'This is why they turned away from Jehovah . . . *"All we like sheep have gone astray; we have turned every one to his own way"* (Isaiah vi. 6) . . . Away from the way of the Lord to their own way.' And their own way was to choose shepherds other than the Lord.

It is also impressive to notice that in Psalm xcv. 7, where the verse begins: *"We are the people of his pasture, and the sheep of his hand"*, it goes on with this strange word: *"To-day, Oh, that ye would hear his voice! Harden not your heart"*. *"We are the . . . sheep of his hand"*—but the sheep can have very hard hearts and refuse to hear the Shepherd's voice. So to His sheep of old He said: *"To-day Oh . . . harden not your heart"*.

Do you know that that very word is quoted at least three times in the Letter to the Hebrews? *"To-day if ye shall hear his voice, harden not your hearts"* (Hebrews iii. 7, 8). So it was hardness of heart, refusal to hear His voice, that lost Israel their Shepherd. Paul says in the Letter to the Romans: *"I would not, brethren, have you ignorant . . . that a hardening in part hath befallen Israel"*

(Romans xi. 25), and you have only to read this chapter, John x, to see the hard heart of Israel. It is a terrible thing!

Just look at it! Jesus has been speaking of Himself as the good Shepherd, who gives His life for the sheep. He has said: "*I give unto them eternal life; and they shall never perish*" (verse 28). There are all these wonderful things about Himself as their Shepherd and about His sheep— and do you notice what happened? "*There arose a division again among the Jews because of these words. And many of them said, He hath a devil*" . . . "*I am the good shepherd . . . I lay down my life for the sheep . . . I came that they may have life . . . I give unto them eternal life; and they shall never perish.*" He has said all these wonderful and beautiful things and the Jews said: "*He hath a devil*"!

Now do you understand why God had to cast them off? 'We have hardened our hearts. We have turned every one to our own way. All we like sheep have gone astray. We have gone away from the Shepherd because of self-will. In other words, we have said: "*We will not that this man reign over us*" (Luke xix. 14).'

That is the Jewish background of this chapter. You can feel the atmosphere of antagonism, and you can feel how they hated Him. Presently they will take counsel that they may kill Him. He was right when He called them wolves who would destroy the sheep!

Jesus came right into that atmosphere and said: 'I am the good Shepherd, and I am going to lead My flock out of this. I am going to take them out of this setting and out of this false flock.' And so He leads the nucleus of His new flock and gives unto them eternal life. He begins with a nucleus out of the old. A dividing work takes place.

I did not read all that the Jews said because I wanted to keep it until now: "*There arose a division again among the*

*Jews because of these words. And many of them said, He hath
a devil, and is mad; why hear ye him? Others said, These are
not the sayings of one possessed with a devil. Can a devil open
the eyes of the blind?"*

Evidently the Lord Jesus is getting some other sheep.
There are those out of the old flock who are inclined
toward Him. They are the new beginning, the new
Israel, and He says: 'I will lead them out, right out of that
whole setting'.

And we see that nucleus on the Day of Pentecost,
beginning with twelve—then one hundred and twenty—
then more than five hundred brethren at once—then
three thousand—and then five thousand. There is the
new flock.

Well, here is Jesus building upon the Old Testament
principle. If He cannot take the Old Testament sheep,
He will take up the principle of shepherd and sheep and
will carry it over into His new Israel of this dispensation.

The position is quite clear, is it not? You have it there
quite plainly. One Israel is being put aside and another
Israel is being put in its place. The earthly is going, the
heavenly is coming in to take its place, and this heavenly
Israel becomes the new flock under the Shepherd.

We have to note some of the marks of these true
sheep. Jesus says in this chapter: *"I know mine own"*, and
there are certain marks by which He knows His own
sheep. If you have any doubt as to whether you are one
of the Lord's sheep, you can prove it, and the Lord
Himself knows by these marks.

You know, shepherds put a mark on their own sheep.
It may be a red mark, or a blue one, but on their sheep
they put their own mark. Jesus is saying here: 'I know
My sheep because there are marks on them.' What are
these marks?

The first one is this: "*My sheep hear my voice*".

You know, this is an illustration of a great truth. The Gospels are but illustrations of great truths. If you go on into the rest of the New Testament you will read a great deal about spiritual intelligence and about spiritual understanding, and about having 'an ear to hear what the Spirit saith'. You have that seven times at the beginning of the Book of the Revelation—"*He that hath an ear, let him hear what the Spirit saith*" (Revelation ii. 7, etc.). Of course, that is not our outward ear. The Lord's sheep have an inward ear given to them, that is, a faculty of spiritual intelligence and an ability to hear what no one else can hear. It was to that that the Lord was referring—'My sheep know when I speak. They have an ear for Me and are always listening for My voice. They hear My voice.'

Every truly born again child of God is given this faculty of spiritual hearing. That is why, in the early days of your Christian life, you say: 'The Lord seems to be saying something to me. He seems to be saying that I ought not to talk as I do, that I ought not to dress as I have been dressing, and that I ought not to go to the places to which I used to go, and many other things like that.' The Lord seems to be saying something to us. He is speaking in the heart, and as we go on in the Christian life that becomes the governing thing in our lives. We seek to hear what the Lord has to say to us, and when we hear His voice a crisis arises. Are we going back to the way of the old Israel? Or are we going to hear that voice and obey?

That is the message of the Letter to the Hebrews: 'Do not go back on to that old ground. Today if ye shall *hear his voice*, harden not your hearts as the old Israel did.' It is a very wonderful thing to see people who are obeying His voice! Other people do not have to tell them these

things. They are a poor kind of Christian who have to
be told all the time what they should do and what they
should not do. The true sheep hear His voice and they
follow Him. It is something that comes out of the
heart—they have heard Him speaking in the heart.

This, of course, is the whole of that New Testament
subject of spiritual understanding, and you and I, as
Christians, are supposed to have that faculty.

We were speaking earlier about Nicodemus. He was
a ruler of the Jews and a great man in Israel. He had a
high position and a great education, and yet he had not
the first idea of spiritual things. Jesus had to say to him:
*"If I told you earthly things, and ye believe not, how shall ye
believe, if I tell you heavenly things?"* (John iii. 12).
Nicodemus could not see beyond the natural to the
spiritual. When Jesus said 'You must be born again', he
could not see beyond the natural, and said: *"How can
a man be born when he is old?"* (John iii. 4). He had no
spiritual intelligence. He was like a little child, although
a great teacher in Israel.

I have a little grand-daughter about four years of age.
She went to Sunday School and when she came home
she said to her mother: 'Mother, will you get out for
me all my baby toys which we put away?' Her mother
said: 'Why do you want your baby toys out again?' 'Oh,'
she said, 'my teacher says I must be born again!'

Well, that is a little child and you might expect that of
her, but here is the great big grown-up Nicodemus and
he is no better than that! You might expect more of him,
but you do not get it. Spiritual intelligence belongs to the
born again ones, and we are given that gift with our new
birth. We have a whole new set of faculties, to hear, to
see, to feel, and so on. And I repeat that it is about that
very thing that the New Testament speaks when spiritual

understanding is mentioned. That is what Jesus meant when He said: "*My sheep hear my voice*".

The next mark of these sheep is: "*My sheep . . . follow me.*"

Those words are simple, but they have a very deep meaning. They mean that His sheep never have to be driven, never have to be compelled to go His way. His sheep follow Him in a voluntary, spontaneous way. The Lord never has to say (or ought never to have to say) to His sheep: 'You *must* go this way.' The Lord is going a certain way and His sheep see which way He is going and follow Him.

Of course, in the western world it is just the other way round where sheep are concerned. Sheep have to be driven, but it is not like that in the East, and Jesus takes the principle of government from the East. He says: 'I don't drive My sheep. I never have to get behind them and force them to go on. I never have to send a dog after them to get them going. My sheep hear My voice and they follow Me.' It is a spontaneous movement of the heart to go after the Lord.

Let us apply the law. These are the marks of the Lord's sheep. Are you one of His sheep? Do you really hear Him speaking in your heart? Do you listen for His voice? Do you seek to have your life guided by that voice of the Spirit within speaking to you through the Word of God, through the circumstances of your life, through your sorrows? The Lord always has something to say to us. There are very few things which happen to the Lord's sheep which do not have some meaning. It is for us to seek to know what it is the Lord is saying to us. The government of the life of the Lord's sheep is by hearing His voice. Do you know anything about that? And what about this spontaneous response to the Lord? Is yours a

heart that readily goes after the Lord? Is it one that has
only to know that the Lord wants something and it
responds with a hearty 'Yes, Lord'?

What is the bond between us, the Lord's sheep, and
Him, the Shepherd? It is the same bond that existed
between the old Israel, with whom the Lord had so much
difficulty, and the Lord. This same principle of His
ownership is taken over. That which unites us with the
Lord is the realization that we belong to Him, that He is
absolute owner of our lives. To quote another Scripture:
"Ye are not your own; for ye were bought with a price"
(I Corinthians vi. 19, 20), and we have the mark of the
Lord put upon us, which is the seal of His ownership.
Paul tells us that the seal is the Holy Spirit—*"Ye were
sealed with the Holy Spirit"* (Ephesians i. 13). When you
look at a seal you know to whom the object belongs.
It says: 'This is the property of a certain person.' The
Lord gives us His Spirit as the seal that we belong to Him.

What a sheep the Apostle Paul was! He said: *"Let no
man trouble me* (that is, try to draw me away): *for I bear
branded on my body the marks of Jesus"* (Galatians vi. 17) . . .
'The marks of Jesus mean that I belong to Him.' He said
on the ship when he was travelling to Rome: *"There
stood by me this night an angel of the God whose I am, whom
also I serve"* (Acts xxvii. 23). The true sheep of the Lord
Jesus are never ashamed to say: 'I belong to the Lord
Jesus. He owns my life and everything that I have. I am
completely committed to Him.' That is a true sheep!

Well, these are the marks of the Lord's new Israel. And
you can now understand why we have these words
which have been the key to our meditation: *"Wherefore,
holy brethren, companions of a heavenly calling . . . companions of Christ"* (Hebrews iii. 1, 14). There is a kind of
companionship between this Shepherd and His sheep.

They are not just animals, they are friends. There is a wonderful friendship between the Lord Jesus and His own—*"Companions of a heavenly calling"*.

CHAPTER FIVE

(xiv) *The Glory of God in Resurrection*

> Reading: John xi
> Ezekiel xxxvii. 12, 13
> Isaiah xi. 11
> Romans ix. 27-29

In order to see the setting of this point it is necessary first to look back to what is marked as chapter x:

"*They sought again to take him (Jesus): and he went forth out of their hand*" (John x. 39).

"*The Jews took up stones again to stone him. . . . The Jews answered him, For a good work we stone thee not, but for blasphemy; and because that thou, being a man, makest thyself God*" (John x. 31, 33).

Then verses 7 and 8 in chapter xi:

"*Then after this he saith to the disciples, Let us go into Judaea again. The disciples say unto him, Rabbi, the Jews were but now seeking to stone thee; and goest thou thither again?*"

You see the Jewish background. Repeatedly the Jews attempted to stone Jesus. They wanted to do with Him what later they did with His servant Stephen—just stone Him, and leave Him there broken in body and dead. Again and again they took up the stones to stone Him—"*They took up stones to cast at him*" (John viii. 59). That is the Jewish background of chapter eleven, and it shows us very clearly why Israel of old had to be set aside, and why God had to have another Israel. That kind of Israel could never serve the purpose of God! And so it was rejected.

If you remove the mark 'Chapter xi' and read through from chapter ten right on, you find that this account of the death and raising of Lazarus is set right in that background. We must never just take some story as an incident in itself. We must always recognize that it relates to something else, and this dying and raising of Lazarus is set right in that Jewish background. This was not just a coincidence, a thing that happened by chance. Jesus made it perfectly clear that it was in the plan of God. If you read the story you will see that it is quite clear from what Jesus said that this is all planned and arranged by God. He arranged that Lazarus should die, and Jesus is not going to interfere with that. It *has* to happen because it stands related to some very big thing that God is doing.

Well, let us look at Lazarus. Lazarus is sick, and it is a sickness for which there is no cure. I do not know how many doctors there were within reach of Bethany, or in Jerusalem, which was just a few miles away, but I am quite sure that if there were any doctors about, the sisters could have sent for one during those four days. But whether they did or not, the doctors could have done nothing. Lazarus just *has* to die in the plan of God. He has a sickness for which there is no cure, and even Jesus, who had raised the dead more than once, will not interfere in this matter. He just positively refuses to prevent Lazarus from dying. It tells us here that when Jesus heard about it He stayed where He was for four days. That, of course, made the great problem for the sisters, and it gave something to the enemies. They said: "*Could not this man, which opened the eyes of him that was blind, have caused that this man also should not die?*" Well, let the sister miss-

D

understand and the enemies misjudge! Jesus is not going to be moved by anything, so He lets Lazarus die.

Is this a hopeless situation? Well, what does Jesus say about it? When He received the message from the sisters He said: "*This sickness is not unto death, but for the glory of God, that the Son of God may be glorified thereby.*" . . . This sickness is not unto *death*, and yet He let him die. He evidently meant: 'This sickness is not unto death for ever. It is not final death.' Later He said "*Lazarus is dead*", and yet He said "*This sickness is not unto death*". So He meant: Death is not going to be the last word.

Now let us note this as we go along: the spiritual knowledge of Jesus. Although He was a long way away from Bethany, He knew exactly when Lazarus died. No one sent Him a second message to say that Lazarus was dead. He said to His disciples: "*Our friend Lazarus is fallen asleep*". They replied: "*If he is fallen asleep, he will recover.*" . . . "*Then Jesus therefore said unto them plainly, Lazarus is dead.*" Jesus knew in His spirit that Lazarus had died, and He always knew in His spirit when there was death and when there was life anywhere.

If the Lord Jesus is in *us* by His Spirit, we always know whether things are alive or dead. We may go amongst some people and say: 'My word, there is no life here! It is dead.' Or we may go amongst others and say: 'Well, there is life here.' We know it in our spirit. No one has to tell us that those people are dead or alive. And that is a mark of the Lord Jesus.

Jesus knew the moment that Lazarus died. Thus we have the Jewish background, the immediate connection of this incident, that is, the connection of the old Israel. That is why I read those Scriptures from Ezekiel and Isaiah. When Israel was in captivity in Babylon and Assyria, the Lord said they were dead and buried, and

He said "*I will open your graves*". To the Lord they were in their graves. And then Isaiah said that a remnant would return, and that remnant was the people who came out of the grave of Assyria and Babylon.

Did you notice that in Romans Paul takes that up and brings it over into the New Testament? He quotes Isaiah's word about a remnant and says that out of the old buried Israel there is going to come a remnant that is resurrected by the Lord, and that remnant is going to be incorporated into the new heavenly Israel.

That is why this story of Lazarus is put right in the Jewish setting. You notice that Jesus deliberately moves into the hostile Jewish area. It was there that they had repeatedly tried to stone Him, but He said to His disciples: "*Let us go into Judaea again.*" They said, 'Lord, they have only recently tried to stone you there. Why go back?' But He would not accept their argument. He deliberately went back into the hostile area although it was so opposed to Him. Why did He do that? The story of Lazarus is the answer. This death and raising of Lazarus was set over against that situation. Right in the midst of the rejected, dead and buried old Israel He is going to raise a new one.

You might have thought that when the Lord wanted to start His new work He would have gone to some other country. He might have said: 'Well, I can do nothing in Jerusalem or in Palestine. Let Me go to India, or to China, and start all over again', but He deliberately went back into Judaea and said: 'In the place of death I am going to have resurrection.'

The Day of Pentecost is wonderful for that fact alone. If ever there was an impossible situation, it was Jerusalem on that day! The old Israel had been rejected by God and was dead from His standpoint. It was buried—and right there God brought in by new birth His new Jerusalem. That is the immediate setting and meaning of this incident.

But we said that Paul carries this whole thing right over into the New Testament and says: 'God has sent the old Israel away, but He is going to bring out of that very place of death His new Israel. A remnant is going to be saved through union with Jesus Christ in death and resurrection.'

What is the new Israel? What are marked chapters nine, ten and eleven in the Letter to the Romans deal, on the one side, with the death of the old Israel, the rejected nation. And then the Apostle says that out of that a remnant will be brought. But you see chapter eleven goes straight into chapter twelve. And what is chapter twelve about? It is about the Body of Christ. And what is that Body? It is not Jew and Gentile brought together, but it is both, having lost their own distinctiveness, becoming one in Christ. In another place Paul says: "*There can be neither Jew nor Greek, there can be neither bond nor free . . . for ye all are one man in Christ Jesus*" (Galatians iii. 28). So that when the old Israel is removed and a remnant is taken out of it, buried with Christ and raised together with Him, it does not come back as a Jewish remnant, but as a part of the Body of Christ. That is the new Israel.

Well, I have said that that is the immediate connection. What will help us most, however, is to see the wider connection.

We go back to Lazarus. The New Testament teaches us this: that the Cross of Jesus Christ does not cure the old man. It crucifies him. That is the trouble with most of us. Let us be perfectly honest about it! We are wanting the Lord to cure our old man, to make him a good old man, and to remove from him all his faults, all that is wrong with him and all his sinful nature. The Cross of the Lord Jesus does not do that. It says: 'In the sight of God the old man is dead and buried.' "*Our old man*", says Paul, "*was crucified with him*" (Romans vi. 6). Jesus never came to any old man to heal him and make him better, and yet we, all the days of our lives, are wanting the Lord to make us better. Right to the end of our lives the old man will still be the old man, but with this difference —that God looks upon him as buried, as in the grave, as crucified with Christ. 'In Christ (risen) there is a new creation.'

That is Lazarus. Jesus would not cure Lazarus of his sickness. And God would not cure Israel of its evil nature. He said: 'It must die!'

That is only half the story, but let us be quite clear about it. There will always be an incurable background in our life and it will not be healed. It is there all the time and will not be cured of its spiritual maladies. Any day, if you like to go back on the ground of the old man, you can commit the same sins. That is what the New Testament teaches on the one side.

But the glory will be in that which stands over against the background. It will be in what is in the foreground. We may have a sick body, for the Lord does not always heal sick bodies. He does sometimes, but not always, even with the very best saints that He has had. We may have a sick human nature—and we all know that is true. We are all the time up against the troubles in one another. 'Oh, if only I could forget what that brother or that sister is in himself or herself, I would have a happy time! But, you know, he is such an awkward man! He loves the Lord and wants the Lord's best, but if you come up against him naturally you don't find him a very easy man to get on with.' Grace does make differences, but it transcends, not eradicates. As in the case of Paul, we shall all be saying at the end of our course: *"Not that I . . . am already made perfect"* (Philippians iii. 12). Perhaps in our last days, before going to the Lord, people will find some difficulties with us. I am not saying that we ought not to lose some of those strong, wrong ways in our lives. Grace can work miracles in our human nature, but if you are looking for the day in this life when you are going to be absolutely free from that nature, you will be disappointed. Perhaps you say: 'That is a very poor Gospel to preach!'

But there is another side to it. You and I can live in the power of the resurrection of the Lord Jesus with a very sick body and with a very poor human nature. Yes, the power of His resurrection can cover so much. The foreground can just be the power of His resurrection. We have to say about some people: 'Well, you know, they are so weak physically. They know so much about sickness, and yet, look at what the Lord enables them to do! It is a miracle how much work they get through! They ought to have been dead long ago, but they go on. Not in their own strength, however. There is another strength that is over their weakness.' Paul said: *"When I am weak, then am I strong"* (II Corinthians xii. 10). The power of Christ's resurrection was overcoming his weakness. He said: *"Most gladly therefore will I rather glory in my weaknesses, that the power of Christ may rest upon me"* (II Corinthians xii. 9). He was speaking of his physical infirmities and of the power of Christ's resurrection.

What is true in the physical realm is true in the spiritual. If we live in ourselves we will give up. Oh, what a lot of infirmities there are in our natures! We are always carrying about a lot of spiritual weaknesses. Do you understand what I mean? What a trouble are these natural infirmities of ours! If ever we say 'I cannot', and then, because we cannot, we say 'I give it up', we have forfeited the greatest blessing of the Christian life. Think of all that the Apostle Paul had to do and to suffer! It was a terrible life that he had to live, from one standpoint. He had infirmity in his body, he had enemies wherever he went and he suffered numerous adversities. He was in the sea a day and a night. He was in nakedness and hunger. He had to travel on foot mile after mile, month after month. So we can gather up all the difficulties in that life, and if ever a man ought to have said 'I cannot go on', that man was Paul! But what did he say? *"I can do all things in him that strengtheneth me"* (Philippians iv. 13). Not 'I can do all things'—Paul would have said 'I can do nothing'—but *"I can do all things in him that strengtheneth me."* There was a day when naturally he despaired of life. He said: *"We ourselves have had the sentence of death within ourselves, that we should not trust in ourselves, but in God which raiseth the dead"* (II Corinthians i. 9—R.V. margin).

Lazarus was absolutely hopeless and helpless. He could do nothing—and that is how we are naturally. But Jesus said that it was *"for the glory of God"*.

Dear friends, the glory of God is manifested in those who in themselves are as good as dead, but whom He enables to go on and do much for Him. Jesus may not always heal us in body or in nature, but He can give us divine life and that is a great thing.

Perhaps some of you have heard of God's great servant, Dr. A. B. Simpson. He was a great believer in divine healing and wrote a book on it. But, in spite of his belief, he said this: 'So that no one will misunderstand my position, I do not say that everyone has to be healed, but I do say that everyone can know divine life, which is something more than natural life.'

Well, back to Lazarus. The Lord did not heal him, but He gave him resurrection life, and that is the hope of everyone. The Lord may want to heal you in your body, or He may not do it. However, whether He does or does not, He does not want us to live on our own life, but by resurrection life. That is what Jesus meant when He said: "*This sickness is not unto death, but for the glory of God*". If you look through your New Testament you will see that God is always glorified in resurrection. That is where the glory of God is.

You may see a very weak Christian physically, but you may glorify God in that one because of the wonderful power of divine life. You may see a person who has many faults and lots of things about them that you do not like, and yet there is something more than that—there is the Lord's life in them. While you may not glory in what they are naturally, you can glorify God for what they are spiritually.

That is the real heart of this incident of Lazarus. Life out of death is God's secret, the thing that glorifies Him most of all.

Is that all a lovely story and wonderful truth? Put it into operation tomorrow morning! Say to the Lord when you get up: 'Lord, I am no good in myself, but I am going to live this day by the power of Your resurrection.' There may be impossible situations inside or outside yourself, but just say to the Lord: 'Now, Lord, you get glory today by enabling me to live in resurrection life.' It is something that we are to take by faith every day.

Timothy was evidently a physically weak young man.

There was something wrong with his stomach and it was constantly troubling him. Paul said: *"Lay hold on the life eternal"* (1 Timothy vi. 12), and spoke of his *"often infirmities"* (I Timothy v. 23). If the Lord meant everyone to be healed physically, why did Paul not heal Timothy? Paul knew that there was something better than being healed physically. The power of eternal life in a weak physical body is a great testimony. *"Lay hold on the life eternal"*—that is resurrection life, and it is something that we have to do.

CHAPTER SIX

(xv) *The Vine of God's Full Satisfaction*

Reading: John xv
Psalm lxxx. 8, 14
Isaiah v. 1, 2
Jeremiah ii. 21, vi. 9
Ezekiel xv. 1-6

The fifteenth step in the transition from the old Israel to the new is here in the fifteenth chapter of the Gospel by John: "*I am the true vine, and my Father is the husbandman.*"

You have the Old Testament background to that in the passages we have read: What Israel was intended to be, failed to be, and their destiny—"*Cast into the fire*". It is clear from these Scriptures that Israel was God's vine, but it became a false vine and God had to cast it into the fire, where it has been for nearly twenty centuries.

But when God cast that vine into the fire, He brought forth another. We have said that this Gospel by John sets forth the putting away of the old and the bringing in of the new. We have seen that various names of the old Israel have been taken over into the new Israel, and here in this chapter the vine is taken over. When Jesus said "I am the true vine", He emphasized that word '*true*'. If you could hear Him saying that phrase, it would be like this: "I am the *true* vine". The implication is perfectly clear. 'I take the place of the false vine. That has been cast away and I am the true vine which takes its place.'

We have to spend a little while seeing how Israel was false to its very nature and purpose.

What is the nature of a vine? For one thing, it spreads out far and wide, on the right and on the left, always reaching out to cover more space. It is not the nature of the vine just to go straight up. It reaches out, expands itself.

Israel was raised up for this very purpose—to stretch out their arms and embrace the nations: "*I . . . will give thee . . . for a light to the Gentiles*" (Isaiah xlii. 6) is the word: "*Nations shall come to thy light, and kings to the brightness of thy rising*" (Isaiah lx. 3). God raised up Israel to be a testimony in the nations, to bring the knowledge of God to the whole world. It was Israel's calling to fulfil a world purpose and a world vision. They were intended to be His missionary nation to the whole world, but instead of embracing the nations, they excluded them. They drew a wall round themselves and said 'We are *the* people and all others are dogs.' They called the Gentiles 'dogs'. They shut themselves in to themselves and became an exclusive people, thus contradicting their own nature and mission. Exclusiveness was a contradiction to the very nature of Israel—and it is *always* a contradiction to divine nature. It is not written in Scripture: 'God so loved the Jewish nation that He gave His only begotten Son.' It says: "God so loved the *world*". The very love of God was contradicted by their exclusiveness. His very nature amongst them was violated in that way: and to turn in upon ourselves is always a violation of divine calling. It is a sin for any people to make themselves an end in themselves. That is why in the order of nature—when nature is normal—a family expands. The Lord laid down this law right at the beginning of human history, when He said to Noah and his sons after the flood: "*Be fruitful and multiply, and replenish the earth*" (Genesis ix. 1). It was in the very nature of things by the appointment of God. As I say, when things are normal, no lives are an end in themselves. Of course, I know of those exceptions when it is not possible to expand, but I am speaking of the *normal* course. In the very nature of things God intends life to be an expanding life. Anyone who violates that law deliberately will be an end in himself or herself and will sin against God's law.

Israel was called to expand and fill the earth with the knowledge of the Lord, but they withheld that knowledge from the nations and turned in on themselves, made themselves an end in themselves. So God came down upon that and said: 'All right! You shall be an end in yourselves.' God's judgments are usually the confirmation of our own choices!

That was Israel's violation of their nature as a vine. Instead of expanding to the world, it contracted into itself and anything like that is always fatal.

What about the purpose? Quite obviously the purpose of a vine is to bear fruit. It bears grapes, and from grapes there is to come the wine. In the Old Testament wine is always a symbol of life. That is why we have it at the Lord's Table. It represents His blood, and in that there is life. He Himself called it the fruit of the vine. He did not say: 'I will no more drink of My blood until that day when I drink it new in the kingdom of God.' What He did say was: "I will no more drink of *the fruit of the vine*, until that day when I drink it new in the kingdom of God" (Mark xiv. 25). The grapes and the wine are symbols of life.

Israel of old was called to minister the life of God to all the nations. When you read these Gospels and look to see what kind of fruit it is that Israel is bearing, you find that it is anything but life. It is really death. The fruit was sour. All those who were tasting the fruit of that Israel were turning away and saying: 'We do not want any more.' It was not life: it was death. The Gospels are just full of that truth.

Jesus said: "*I am the true vine*" ... "*In him was life: and the life was the light of men*" (John i. 4). Men's faces grew light when they tasted *Him*.

Did you notice one thing about the vine that we read in the Old Testament? We read, in Ezekiel xv, that the vine has no other purpose in its existence than to bear fruit. Have you ever seen anything made of vine? You have never seen a table, or a vessel or even a walking-stick made of vine! Ezekiel says that you can do nothing with the wood of the vine—you cannot even make from it a peg on which to hang things. The vine is absolutely useless apart from the fruit. The grapes are the only purpose of its existence, and if it does not bear them, then, says Ezekiel, you just cast it into the fire. There are no by-products of the vine, no secondary use. It exists for one thing, and one thing only, and that is fruit.

God raised up the old Israel to bear His divine fruit of life and light for the nations, but they failed to do that. God had no other use for an Israel like that, so He said 'Cast it into the fire.' He did that nearly twenty centuries ago and that is where Israel is now.

We can see from that what the Lord Jesus means when He says that He is the true vine and we are the branches. The *true* vine is that which fulfils the one and only purpose of its existence.

So Jesus brings this illustration over to Himself and His Church, and it is perfectly clear what is the nature of the Lord Jesus. He is reaching out to all men, embracing the whole world. He asks *all* the nations into His heart. *All* men are His concern and not any one nation. He said to His disciples: "Go ye therefore, and make disciples of *all the nations*" (Matthew xxviii. 19). It is the very nature of Jesus to do that. It is quite foreign to Him to be exclusive, small and narrow and self-occupied.

Our salvation is to have our hearts enlarged so that they are bigger than ourselves. Anyone who turns in on himself or herself, and those who are always occupied with themselves, are dying while they live. It cannot be avoided. Let a little company of the Lord's people live just to itself, become wholly occupied with itself, and its days are numbered. They are living a living death. Their destiny is to fade out. That is true of any one Christian or of any company of the Lord's people, because Christ is in the believer and His very nature is to reach out like the vine. He would draw all men unto Himself, and for His people to be otherwise is a contradiction to His very nature, which is the nature of the true vine.

Jesus says: "*I am the vine, ye are the branches*". The branches of the vine make one vine—they partake of the same nature. Do you notice that it is the very branches themselves that do the expanding work of Jesus? Yes, this expanding work is manifested by the branches.

That, of course, is what happened in Jerusalem right at the beginning, when some troubles sprang up in the Christian church there. It was the first bit of trouble that the Christian church had! Some of the first Apostles wanted to stay in Jerusalem and build up the church there. Forgetting the commandment of the Lord, they were just settling down to make Jerusalem the centre of everything and the church an exclusive body. Then there rose up in their midst a young man "*full of faith*

and of the Holy Spirit" (Acts vi. 5), and his name was
Stephen. If you listen to what Stephen said you will
recognize that what he is saying has this meaning: 'This
will not do. We have been called for the nations. We are
not to be an exclusive people. We are called to a world
mission and must not settle down in the old Judaism.'
Some of the first Christians and Christian leaders did not
agree with him. Of course, the old Israel did not agree
with that! And so they stoned Stephen on this very issue
of the world mission of the Church. I cannot help asking
the question: Where were James and Peter when Stephen
was being stoned? They were in Jerusalem, but were not
present. Why was it that Stephen was stoned and not
Peter or James? Because at that time they were not taking
the line that Stephen was taking. They were making
Jerusalem everything, and, of course, the old Israel would
not stone them for doing that, so they were quite safe
somewhere in Jerusalem. But Stephen was stoned.

Do understand that there is something here of which
to take note: that this new Israel is given a mission to all
the nations, and there is a great price to pay for that. The
whole kingdom of Satan is against it. If you will just
become a little, quiet, compromising local sect you will
be all right. The devil won't worry you if you are just
living within your own walls and closed doors, and the
world will not trouble about you. It will leave you
alone . . . but if you go out on this heavenly level of
things and embrace all men in Christ, you will find that
the world is against you and the devil is against you. You
and I ought to see this in our day as no one has ever seen
it before. Do you not see what is happening in the nations?
There is not a missionary left in China! It is no longer
possible for one to go into that country; and that same
thing is happening in other parts of the world. They have

tried to drive them out of Africa. Why is this? Oh, the kingdom of Satan does not want Jesus to get into his world. There have been literally many thousands of martyrs for Jesus Christ in China, and many others in Africa, and in other parts. It has never been quite like this before. It is a new phase of things. Satan knows that his time is short and that he must do all he can to close the nations to Jesus Christ. So there is a great price bound up with this world mission. Stephen is the great example of that.

The purpose, then, of Christ and His Church, of the vine and the branches, is to bring life to men all over this world.

I wonder if that is altogether true of the church today! Do you not think that even the Christian Church is failing in this matter? It is not really bringing life to the nations. Many a place called a 'church' is not bringing life even to its own little locality. This is a contradiction of Christ!

But it is all very well to think of this objectively. It has to come down to every one of us. What is the proof that Christ is in you and in me? How can it be known that Christ is in us? Only in one way—that others are receiving life through us, that we minister the life of Christ to others, that when hungry and needy people come into touch with us they feel the touch of life. They may express it in different ways, but it amounts to this: 'That man, that woman, has something that I have not got and it is something that I need. There is something about them that I feel, and it is what I really need.' That should be true of every Christian because Christ is in us, expanding Himself through us and ministering His life through us.

Oh, do pray, dear friends, every day as you get up: 'Lord, make me a channel of life to someone today. Lord,

minister Your own life through me to someone today.
May I bring life wherever I am.' The Lord has no other
purpose for you and for me. We may try to do a lot of
things, but if we belong to the Vine we are no good for
anything but to bear fruit; and that is to bring life to
others. We are not even to be a peg upon which to hang
something, or a walking-stick to help someone to stand
up straight. No, God has no use for us other than to bear
fruit, to bring life.

Jesus said here in this chapter: *"Every branch that
beareth fruit, he cleanseth it, that it may bear more fruit"*. Of
course, we understand that in nature and agree with it.
Perhaps if you have had anything to do with grape vines,
you have done it yourself. It is strange that we believe
in it as a law of nature and say: 'It is the right and the best
thing to do to cut this piece off so that it will do better',
but we do not agree with the Lord doing it to us. When
He begins to do it we are full of grumbles and complaints!
When for a little while He calls us to do less in order that
He might fit us to do more, we do not agree. When it
seems that the Lord is taking away some of our fruit,
some of our work, we are full of problems. We do not
understand the Lord and begin to ask questions about
His love.

Jesus has laid this down as a positive truth. Here is some
branch that is bearing fruit (not one that is bearing no
fruit: that, He says, will be cast into the fire) and it is
that one that He prunes. Here is a branch that is fulfilling
its vocation and the Lord looks at it. He says: 'That is very
good! I am very pleased with it, but I can do better, and
there is better that that branch can do.' So He takes the
knife, and He disciplines us, He reduces us in order to
increase us. He cuts some away in order that there might
be more.

E

What a lot of history there is in that statement! The
writer of the Letter to the Hebrews said: "*All chastening
seemeth for the present to be not joyous, but grievous: yet
afterward it yieldeth peaceable fruit unto them that have been
exercised thereby, even the fruit of righteousness*" (Hebrews
xii. 11). That is only saying in another way that the
Husbandman does sometimes take the knife and He cuts
deeply into our souls, but afterward there is more and
better fruit than there was before.

Now we come to this last word. The wine comes from
the grape through the winepress, which is the symbol of
pressure. What pressure is brought to bear upon that
fruit in order to get the wine! The winepress is the symbol
of breaking, and that fruit is broken to pieces. The wine
is wrung out of its agony.

The Lord Jesus said "I am the true Vine", and it was
prophesied of Him that He would tread the winepress
alone. The Cross was His winepress. How He was
pressed in the Cross! He was crushed and broken, but
out of that breaking has come the life which you and I
have, and which so many in all the nations have received.
That is true, in a measure, of His Church. It was out of
the breaking and crushing of the Church that the life
came to the world. And that is true of every member,
every branch of the vine. If we are to fulfil this true,
living ministry, it will only be through suffering, through
the winepress, through pressure and through breaking.
Paul said: "*We were pressed out of measure, above strength*"
(II Corinthians i. 8—A.V.)—but what life has come out
of that man's pressure! It is like that. We are not talking
about preaching and Bible teaching, but about this great
ministry of Christ giving His life through us. It may be
passed on to others through preaching, or through teaching, or through living, but if it is His life it will come out

of experiences of suffering. A preacher or a teacher who has never suffered will never minister life.

Well, this may not seem a very pleasant outlook, but it is true. The best doctors and nurses are those who know something about suffering themselves. Some are just professional, treating you as a case—you are just case No. —. But, ah! there are others who treat you as a person, a human being, who care for you. If you ask why, you may find that they have a background of suffering themselves. They know just a little of what you are going through. We have read in the Letter to the Hebrews: "*We have not a high priest that cannot be touched with the feeling of our infirmities; but one that hath been in all points tempted like as we are . . . he is able to succour them that are tempted*" (Hebrews iv. 15, ii. 18). He has been the way of the winepress and we have received the benefit.

Is this why Paul said: "*That I may know him . . . and the fellowship of his sufferings*" (Philippians iii. 9)? He knew quite well that the sufferings of Christ meant life, and if there was one thing which Paul wanted for others, it was that they should have this life, and have it through him. So he said: "*That I may know . . . the fellowship of his sufferings*".

That may not be our ambition, and we may not like the idea very much, but may the Lord help us to look at things in this way: 'The Lord is putting me in the winepress. He is putting me through a time of great pressure. I am being broken and crushed. Therefore the Lord intends to have more fruit, more life, and more people to have the life.' It is the very nature of this thing to reach out to others. That is the *true* vine. Anything that is not like that is the false vine.

"*I am the vine, ye are the branches.*"

CHAPTER SEVEN

(xvi) *The High Priest of the Israel of God*

Reading: John xiii. 1-16

If there were space I would turn you to the Old Testament and we would read together four passages which relate to the making and setting up of the laver in the court of the tabernacle. You will remember that the Lord commanded Moses to make a laver of brass and it was to be placed right at the centre of the outer court. It was to be filled with water and there the priests were to wash their hands and their feet before they entered into the holy place. Although it does not say so, it is very probable that they washed one another's feet. Whether that was true or not—and I think it was—this laver was for such washing in relation to the sacrifice.

Here in the thirteenth chapter of John the Lord Jesus is acting in the capacity of the priest; in the seventeenth chapter is what is universally called the high priestly prayer of the Lord Jesus. There is so much in that prayer which is taken up from the thirteenth chapter—"*Sanctify them in the truth . . . for their sakes I sanctify myself, that they themselves also may be sanctified in truth.*"

So in chapter thirteen we have the Priest taking the water and washing the feet of His brothers—His brother priests. He is doing it in the light of a coming day. He said: "*What I do thou knowest not now; but thou shalt understand hereafter*", and afterward it became quite clear that all

the Lord's people are priests. All are called into the sacred
ministry of priesthood.

That is a very large subject, and I can do no more than
just state the truth and leave it there for the time being.

What is the very heart of this chapter? It is in verse
eight: "*Jesus answered him, If I wash thee not, thou hast no
part with me.*" Now we are back with our word in the
Letter to the Hebrews which is rightly translated 'Companions': "We are become *companions* of Christ". These
words "part with me" are from the same root as that
word "companions". Jesus is saying here: 'Unless I wash
you, you can never become My companions. It is those
whose feet I have washed who are My companions of the
heavenly way.'

The companions of Jesus must have clean feet. In His
prayer He made it perfectly clear what that means: "*They
are not of the world, even as I am not of the world*" (John xvii.
16) . . . "*I pray not that thou shouldest take them from the
world, but that thou shouldest keep them from the evil one*"
(John xvii. 15). The companions of Jesus are those whose
feet symbolically are separated and cleansed from the
world.

This world lies under a curse, under the judgment of
God. It is an evil world and the Lord does not want His
companions to be entangled in it, so His work for us is
to separate us from it. Feet mean contact with the earth,
and the Lord Jesus would break that contact where His
own companions are concerned. If we want to be companions of Christ, we must be delivered from this present
evil world. Contact with it means death, defilement. It is
a world that is against the Lord Jesus. The Lord is saying
here in this symbolic act: 'My companions are not of this
world.' He has done it in Himself once for all.

Of course, there is far more in this than I am able to say

at present, but we all know how true this is. Jesus has not
taken us out of the world. We are here and surrounded by
defilement. It is indeed a sinful world! The Lord Jesus
would have us delivered from it, and He has done the
work by which we can be separated from its evil.

That opens up the whole subject of sanctification, but
for our purpose it just explains that word in Hebrews iii. 1:
"Wherefore, *holy* brethren" . . . 'Brethren who are sanctified', which means separated, 'unto God'. Such are the
companions of Christ and of the heavenly calling.

But the Lord Jesus also instituted a ministry for His
companions. He said: "*I have given you an example, that ye
also should do as I have done to you.*" He was saying, in other
words: 'You must help one another to keep clear of the
spirit of this world.' The word which explains that is:
"*Brethren, even if a man be overtaken in any trespass, ye which
are spiritual, restore such a one in a spirit of meekness*" (Galatians vi. 1). The meekness of Jesus in this act offended
Peter: 'You, Lord and Master, getting down on your
knees and washing my feet! I could not think of it—I
could not allow it. I cannot let you humiliate yourself like
that!' . . . "*Ye which are spiritual, restore such a one in a spirit
of meekness.*"

You and I have to learn more about this. It is a spiritual
ministry that is very much needed. There are bodies of
Christians in this world who practise this literally and
have it as part of their service to wash one another's feet.
Well, we will not discuss whether they are right or wrong.
I think, though, that you might wash someone's feet
literally and not do it spiritually. You might wash someone's feet literally and then go away and talk about their
faults and their weaknesses to someone else. I think we are
too much accustomed to pointing out the dirt that is on
people's feet rather than removing it. Our criticisms and

our condemnations of one another! It does not need an expert to see the spiritual uncleanness of people and the touch of this world upon them. Anyone can see their faults.

What are we going to do? Talk about them? Point them out to other people? Keep them always in view? Allow our attitudes toward them to be influenced by these faults?

If you read through these Gospels you will see that the disciples had plenty of uncleanness on their feet. They quarrelled as to who should be greater in the Kingdom of Heaven and strove together to have the first place. It is all an unpleasant story! They had plenty of faults and failings. Their feet were indeed tainted by this world, but what does it say here about the attitude of Jesus? Such men as they were, yet . . . *"Having loved his own which were in the world, he loved them unto the end"*, and to show His love He humbled Himself. He laid aside the garment of His own glory and took the form of a bondservant. He girded Himself with a towel—the symbol of humble service. He did not say: 'Oh, what a lot of dirt you have on your feet!'—He washed it away.

Then He said: *"I have given you an example, that ye should do as I have done to you"*—'You are priests unto God. Take the water of the laver and wash one another's feet. Only thus can you be companions of the holy place, of the heavenly calling.'

Do you notice that there is a blessing attached to this? It is in verse seventeen: *"If ye know these things, blessed are ye if ye do them."* So there is a blessing attached to washing one another's feet!

SeedSowers
P.O. Box 3317
Jacksonville, FL 32206
800-228-2665

904-598-3456 (fax)   www.seedsowers.com

REVOLUTIONARY BOOKS ON CHURCH LIFE

AN INTRODUCTION TO THE DEEPER CHRISTIAN LIFE

CLASSICS ON THE DEEPER CHRISTIAN LIFE

IN A CLASS BY THEMSELVES

The chronicles of the door *(Edwards)*

The Beginning 8.99
The Escape 8.99
The Birth 8.99
The Triumph 8.99
The Return 8.99

The works of T. Austin-Sparks

The Centrality of Jesus Christ 19.95
The House of God 29.95
Ministry 29.95
Service 19.95

Comfort and healing

A Tale of Three Kings *(Edwards)* 8.99
The Prisoner in the Third Cell *(Edwards)* 5.99
Letters to a Devastated Christian *(Edwards)* 5.95
Healing for those who have been Crucified by Christians *(Edwards)* 8.95
Dear Lillian *(Edwards)* 5.95

Other books on church life

Climb the Highest Mountain *(Edwards)* 9.95
The Torch of the Testimony *(Kennedy)* 14.95
The Passing of the Torch *(Chen)* 9.95
Going to Church in the First Century *(Banks)* 5.95
When the Church was Young *(Loosley)* 14.95
Church Unity *(Litzman, Nee, Edwards)* 14.95
Let's Return to Christian Unity *(Kurosaki)* 14.95

Christian Living

Final Steps in Christian Maturity *(Guyon)* 12.95
Turkeys and Eagles *(Lord)* 8.95
Beholding and Becoming *(Coulter)* 8.95
Life's Ultimate Privilege *(Fromke)* 7.00
Unto Full Stature *(Fromke)* 7.00
All and Only *(Kilpatrick)* 7.95
Adoration *(Kilpatrick)* 8.95
Release of the Spirit *(Nee)* 5.00
Bone of His Bone *(Huegel)* 8.95
Christ as All in All *(Haller)* 9.95

* call for a free catalog 800-228-2665